'A wonderfully clear and concise account of everything you needed to know about inflation which should be read by every citizen.' — **Mervyn King**, former governor of the Bank of England

'Over the past few years, as the cost-of-living crisis has forced many to choose between eating and heating, people have woken up to the huge social as well as economic costs that can be caused by inflation. In this important book, which should be read by those of all political persuasions, Lord Griffiths challenges policy-makers and central banks not to underestimate the serious ethical and moral issues raised.' — **Rt Hon Ruth Kelly**, former Labour Cabinet Minister in the Blair and Brown governments

'Drawing on his extensive experience in academia, government and the world of finance, Lord Griffiths's *Inflation Is About More Than Money* combines monetary pragmatism and ethics to examine the history and perils of inflation. This timely book will appeal both to a general readership and an expert audience.' — **Professor Rosa Lastra**, Sir John Lubbock Chair in Banking Law, CCLS, Queen Mary University of London

'The central point of Brian Griffiths's fine and passionate polemic is that inflation is a moral disease, not just a technical problem. It creates a culture of broken promises that dissolves the social ties necessary for society to cohere and for enterprise to flourish. A policy adviser to Margaret Thatcher, Griffiths draws on the lessons of the 1970s, 1980s and the recent inflation to offer a timely warning to our own world of Covid-19 lockdowns, military buildups and soaring food and energy prices.' — **Lord (Robert) Skidelsky**, Emeritus Professor of Political Economy, University of Warwick

'Brian Griffiths brings to the contemporary policy debate the perspective of one present at the heart of government during the previous inflationary storm. This insightful book is a powerful reminder that the recipe for a monetary inflation works as well today as it ever did. And that the task of bringing inflation under control is no less costly and painful with the passage of time.' — **Peter Warburton**, Director of Economic Perspectives Ltd

'Inflation is caused by "too much money chasing too few goods". But Brian Griffiths asks: Where does "too much money" come from, and why? This clearly written, jargon-free, concise account identifies the several and sometimes distant causes of the social and fiscal conditions that produce too much money. This is a very serious and accessible statement that should be read by politicians and economists, and indeed by anyone who would like to better understand our current and continuing predicament.' — **Forrest Capie**, Emeritus Professor, Bayes Business School, University of London

'Money is ubiquitous in our lives both as an opportunity and a problem. Generations have tried to get some grip on its nature and its effect on our lives and societies. Professor Lord Brian Griffiths, who has spent much of his academic career and his time as adviser to politicians at the highest level in understanding monetary matters, has now distilled his knowledge and experience in this book. A unique feature of the book is the author's approach, as a committed Christian, to thinking about inflation as a moral issue. Accessibly written, it is an informative way to get to know about money and its good and troublesome aspects.' — **Professor Lord Meghnad Desai**

'Brian Griffiths has been tough-minded on inflation and the causes of inflation for half a century. His analysis of the post-Covid resurgence of inflation proves that he has lost none of his bite. I am extremely proud to have helped unleash this brilliant book, which began as a series of essays for *TheArticle*, upon the world. *Inflation Is About More Than Money* should be compulsory reading for all politicians, central bankers and the next generation of economists.' — **Daniel Johnson**, Editor of *TheArticle*

'In a radically uncertain world, the role of politics and policy is to absorb shocks and provide a measure of stability. With intellectual verve and acuity, Brian Griffiths has given us an ethically informed vision that fuses sound money with greater economic justice. A seminal contribution to rethink national renewal from one of Britain's most eminent economists.' — **Adrian Pabst**, Professor of Politics, University of Kent

INFLATION IS ABOUT MORE THAN MONEY

The Centre for Enterprise, Markets and Ethics

We are a think tank based in Oxford that seeks to promote an enterprise, market economy built on ethical foundations.

We undertake research on the interface of Christian theology, economics and business. Our aim is to argue the case for an economy that generates wealth, employment, innovation and enterprise within a framework of calling, integrity, values and ethical behaviour, leading to the transformation of the business enterprise and contributing to the relief of poverty.

We publish a range of material, hold events and conferences, undertake research projects and speak and teach in our areas of concern. We are independent and a registered charity entirely dependent on donations for our work. Our website is www.theceme.org.

For further information please contact the CEME's director, Revd Dr Richard Turnbull, at

The Centre for Enterprise, Markets and Ethics
First Floor
31 Beaumont Street
Oxford OX1 2NP

INFLATION IS ABOUT MORE THAN MONEY

Economics, Politics and the Social Fabric

Brian Griffiths

Copyright © 2025 by Brian Griffiths and Centre for Enterprise, Markets and Ethics

Published by the Centre for Enterprise, Markets and Ethics (https://theceme.org/) in association with the Institute of Economic Affairs (https://iea.org.uk/) and London Publishing Partnership (www.londonpublishingpartnership.co.uk)

All rights reserved

ISBN: 978-1-910666-25-8 (pbk)
ISBN: 978-1-910666-27-2 (ePDF)
ISBN: 978-1-910666-28-9 (ePUB)

A catalogue record for this book is available from the British Library

Typeset in Adobe Garamond Pro by T&T Productions Ltd, London
www.tandtproductions.com

Printed and bound by CPI Group (UK) Ltd, Croydon, CR0 4YY

For Rachel, with love and admiration

Contents

Preface	xi
Acknowledgements	xv
Part I: Background	1
1 Wars, Covid and Ukraine	3
Part II: Why inflation is a Bad Thing	13
2 Real economic costs	15
3 Heating or eating: the cost of living crisis	23
4 Inflation as deceit	31
5 A culture of distrust	41
6 'Things fall apart'	49
Part III: What Went Wrong	57
7 Inflation is always and everywhere a monetary phenomenon	59
8 The case for pragmatic monetarism	69
9 Why did central bankers get it so wrong?	77
Part IV: Catching a Tiger by the Tail	85
10 'Greedflation' and price ceilings	87
11 The cost of controlling inflation	91
Part V: Building Defences Against Future Inflation	101
12 Fiscal discipline for sound money	103

13 What lessons should the Bank of England learn from the current inflation?	115
14 Cultural headwinds in fighting inflation	127
Conclusion: lessons for the future	141
About the author	145
Notes	147
Index	159
Complete list of CEME publications	165

Preface

The response of the government and the Bank of England to the Covid-19 pandemic of 2020 triggered the recent UK inflation. Few people expected it.[1] The scale of the government's response to the pandemic was unexpected: a massive increase in public spending that led to the greatest ever peacetime public sector borrowing, interest rates at almost zero and a rapid increase in the stock of money. The lockdowns instigated by the government in response to the pandemic reduced output, disrupted trade and created shortages. They, too, were unexpected. The current inflation was well underway before the Russian invasion of Ukraine in February 2022, which is again something that was not widely expected.

Most people today under the age of sixty have no memory of living through inflation. This includes all current Cabinet members; many MPs; most civil servants and special advisers; most Bank of England staff; the editors of many newspapers, radio and television news and current affairs programmes; and nearly all bloggers. They have no memory of the political struggle to bring inflation under control or the economic costs of doing so: during the first government of Margaret Thatcher, the Bank of England base rate (commonly referred to as Bank Rate) had to be raised to 17% in November 1979 and unemployment exceeded 3 million by 1982. Friedrich von Hayek, winner of the Nobel Memorial Prize in Economic Sciences, likened conquering inflation to 'catching a tiger by the tail'.

In August 2020, just six months after the first Covid lockdown was announced, I wrote a comment piece for *TheArticle* entitled 'The spectre of inflation',[2] which raised the question of whether in light of the 'staggering increase in public spending and the monetary authorities' rapid monetary expansion' – as well as the rising prices of gold, silver, industrial metals, oil, fine wines, contemporary art and Michael Jordan's old shoes – we were heading for a serious inflation. I pointed out that inflation was a monetary phenomenon; that it involved a real cost to the economy; and that during the high-inflation period in the 1970s, interest rates had needed to be raised to 17% to bring inflation under control. The consequences of inflation had become mistaken for its cause, with the result that a witch hunt began to find guilty parties: trade unions, businesses, foreigners, estate agents, speculators, bankers and traders were all blamed.

We live in a world of unexpected events – a world of radical uncertainty. This is a state of affairs in which it is impossible to assign probabilities to future events. It is this that distinguishes uncertainty from risk. With risk it is possible to calculate the probabilities of future events, so that markets for insurance can develop that offer people protection. The major events that have driven excess money creation – such as Covid-19, lockdowns, the furlough scheme, supply shortages, record government borrowing, the Russian invasion of Ukraine – have all stemmed from uncertainty. Far from being a 'transitory' phenomenon – as the Bank of England, the US Federal Reserve and the European Central Bank, the world's three leading central banks, have argued – the recent inflation has proved to be much stronger and much more persistent than was forecast, which has changed the public's expectations of future inflation and led to the prospect of continued stagflation.

The public hate inflation. It hurts their standard of living. Prices are rising while their incomes are not. Real wages are falling. The cost of living crisis has been extremely painful for many, and those on lower incomes have suffered disproportionately. A major study conducted through surveys of public opinion in the United States, Germany and Brazil by Nobel winner Robert Shiller found that those interviewed typically responded with comments such as 'the economy could collapse', 'inflation makes us feel good but ultimately deceives us', 'it harms economic growth', 'it can cause political chaos, even anarchy', and 'the social atmosphere created by inflation is selfish and harmful to national morale'.[3] Research undertaken for the Bank of England in 2001 concluded that 'a large body of public opinion research has shown that across a diverse array of countries, individual citizens generally have a strong aversion to inflation'.[4]

While economists have focused on the causes of inflation and the cost of bringing it under control, the social consequences of inflation have been less thoroughly explored. When inflation takes off, people become suspicious of anyone and everyone: grasping shopkeepers, companies jacking up prices, militant trade unions demanding higher wages and threatening strikes, landlords increasing rents, and so on. Frequently, the consequences of inflation are mistaken for their cause. This culture of distrust has a corrosive effect on society and undermines the legitimacy of the institutions of both capitalism and liberal democracy.

Inflation raises serious ethical and moral issues. Economic life has evolved from barter to money economies. Western liberal democracies are market economies, and they are successful because people are prepared to hold money on trust. The public's expectation is that the value of money and what it will buy will remain relatively stable from year to year. Inflation undermines that trust and, in turn, it undermines those institutions that have responsibility for it: namely, central banks, banks and central governments. At its root, inflation is a deceit. It is no different from theft. Inflation is a regressive tax, which is not subject to debate and legislation by parliament.

While the UK has never experienced hyperinflation, we have experienced serious inflation. I lived through the inflation of the tumultuous years of the 1970s, when inflation reached 27% in 1975. I was teaching monetary economics at the London School of Economics at the time. The seriousness of inflation was not just an economic cost and a squeeze on the cost of living for everyone: more importantly, it eroded the fabric of our society, creating uncertainty, anxiety and conflict and undermining the legitimacy of ordinary business, banks and the Bank of England.

As with previous inflations, this inflation has lasting lessons to teach us. First, inflation imposes a real cost on economic life. This is something that has been underestimated by economists: because of inflation, a country will be poorer than it would otherwise have been. Much of the cost of inflation is hidden, unlike the cost of unemployment, which is visible. Second, inflation leads to an arbitrary redistribution of income and wealth that achieves no useful purpose but increases wealth inequality. Third, inflation creates a culture of suspicion and distrust that provokes division, social disorder and conflict.

These effects lead people to question the legitimacy of free market economies and liberal democracies, as well as the value of freedom itself. In parliamentary democracies the only safeguard against the destruction that inflation brings are the values people hold. These values underpin the rule of law, property rights and the conventions of liberal democracy. However, such values must be sought outside of the realm of money and economics.

These are the themes I wish to explore in this short book. The first chapter focuses on the historic background of inflation over 250 years and on the role of wars. The next five chapters consider the economic and social costs of inflation, its impact on the culture of everyday life and the way in which it undermines market economies and democratic institutions. Chapters 7–9 explore what we mean by inflation being a monetary phenomenon and look at why central banks failed to recognize that inflation was more than something 'transitory'. After examining the cost of controlling inflation – 'catching a tiger by the tail' – we then in chapters 12–14 look at how we can build defences against future inflation through stronger fiscal rules and a more independent central bank, and we assess the headwinds we face from the changing culture of the society in which we now live.

Acknowledgements

This book grew out of an article, 'The spectre of inflation', that I wrote in the summer of 2020, just after the end of the first UK Covid-19 lockdown. It was originally suggested and eventually published by Daniel Johnson, the editor of *TheArticle*, in August 2020. Daniel encouraged me to write further pieces, so I did, and I can honestly say that without Daniel's constant encouragement this book would never have been written.

I also owe a huge debt to Joanna Moriarty, former publishing editor at SPCK, for encouraging me to write more on economics and ethics even though she knew she might have reservations about the result. John Lenton, who has a background in business and business education, has been a huge support in discussing the substance of the book, and his comments have invariably been helpful.

Together with Joanna and John, Forrest Capie, Charles Goodhart, Charles Eve, Peter Warburton, Stephen Beer, Frank Field, Nigel Biggar, Richard Godden and Carl Ferenbach read and commented on an earlier draft of the book, for which I am most grateful. I am especially indebted to Mervyn King and George Bridges for discussing issues of policy regarding inflation and to other colleagues who were members of the cross-party House of Lords Select Committee on Economic Affairs. Richard Turnbull, the director of the Centre for Enterprise, Markets and Ethics, has been a constant encouragement. The views expressed in the text are, however, entirely my own.

I owe a huge debt to Ewa Pirog, my personal assistant, for her patience, hard work and advice.

Finally, I can never fully express my debt to Rachel, my wife. With her LSE background in sociology and her understanding that economics is a social science that cannot be divorced from larger issues relating to ethics and society, her advice has been invaluable.

PART I

BACKGROUND

CHAPTER 1

Wars, Covid and Ukraine

History is an interesting lens through which to view inflation. Over the last 250 years, taking us back roughly to the beginning of industrialization, there has never been a period of sustained inflation or hyperinflation in the United Kingdom.[1] Before the present inflation there were five periods of serious inflation, four of which were directly associated with wars: the Seven Years' War (1756–63), the French Revolutionary and Napoleonic Wars (1792–1815), World War I (1914–18) and World War II (1939–45).

Even the 1970s inflation (1972–82) had its roots indirectly in the Vietnam War (1965–72), as sterling was pegged to the dollar and the price of the dollar was pegged to gold (see figure 1). The result was that UK inflation followed the rising US rate of inflation until 1971, when the peg was cut. This inflation was then subsequently overshadowed by the 'Barber boom' of 1972–3, which transformed the scale and severity of inflation imported from the United States into something altogether greater.

The government response to the Covid-19 pandemic was not a military campaign, but the disease was an enemy against which the government had to declare war. Initial estimates of total deaths from the pandemic, by reputable research institutions such as Imperial College London, were huge: in the range 345,000–580,000. Each of the lockdowns the government instituted put the UK economy and society on a war footing. The enemy was an invisible, but deadly and resourceful, virus. The battlefields were our hospitals, care homes and social gatherings. The ammunition factories were the country's research labs, universities and pharmaceutical companies. The vaccines were the weapons needed to win the war. The government's response – lockdowns, travel restrictions, social distancing, limits to personal freedom – made unparalleled demands on both the economy and personal freedom, far outstripping anything the United Kingdom had experienced in either of the world wars.

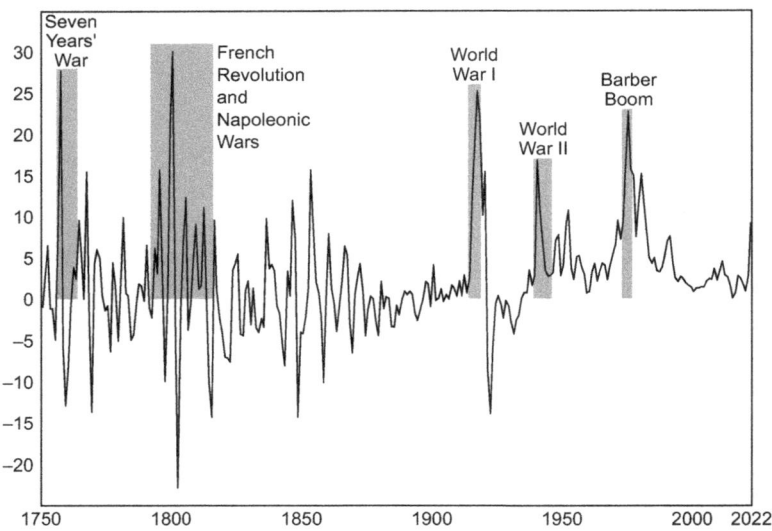

Figure 1. UK consumer price inflation (percentage change). (*Source*: based on data from the Bank of England's Research Dataset 'A millennium of macroeconomic data for the UK'.)

The war against Covid has in many ways been similar to previous military campaigns conducted by government, and it is worthwhile looking briefly at each of these.

THE REVOLUTIONARY AND NAPOLEONIC WARS (1792–1815)

During the first five years of these wars, government spending increased almost threefold, and 90% of the total borrowing came from private investors. The Bank of England increased the note issue and bought government stock paid for by depleting its gold reserves. The national debt relative to gross domestic product (GDP) doubled between 1793 and 1798, and at its peak it reached 268% of GDP.[2] A new tax, income tax, was introduced for the first time in the 1798 budget. After an invasion by a small French force off the Welsh coast at Fishguard in 1797, the government decided to suspend the convertibility of paper money into gold.

The price indices showed great volatility throughout this period, but the trend was clear: prices had risen by around 60% over the course of the wars. Convertibility was eventually restored in 1821 and, following a period of deflation, there was no further sustained period of inflation in the United Kingdom in the nineteenth century. Prices rose in the initial phase of trade cycles but then fell in later phases.

One puzzle is why Britain was forced off the gold standard during the Napoleonic Wars while France remained on a bimetallic standard for their duration.[3] Bordo and White suggest that the issue could be explained as follows:

> The French Revolution's use of confiscation, capital levies and an inflation tax destroyed its credibility and forced Napoleonic France to rely primarily on taxation. In contrast to France's frequent changes in political regime, Britain's continuous parliamentary form of government, in which debt holders exercised considerable influence, was able to issue a massive quantity of debt and leave the gold standard with the promise of eventual redemption.[4]

WORLD WAR I (1914–18)

The average rate of inflation in the fifteen or so years before World War I was 0.47%. That period was followed by a serious inflation during and immediately after the war. Prices more than doubled between 1914 and 1920. These were years in which there was a huge increase in public spending: the national debt rose from £650 million in 1913 to £8,000 million in 1920, and the ratio of government spending to GDP (excluding interest payments) reached 70% by 1919.

The monetary base (notes, coins and commercial bank reserves) more than doubled, from £245 million at the beginning of 1914 to £697 million by the end of 1918, while the money supply also more than doubled. The UK government relied more on borrowing than taxation to finance the war, even though David Lloyd George, the Chancellor of the Exchequer at the time, doubled the income tax rate in November 1914. The money markets for Treasury and commercial bills were large and they played an important role in financing the war effort.[5]

The deficit fell to £326 million in 1919–20 and then moved sharply into a surplus of £230 million in 1920–21 which led to a serious recession and a rise in unemployment to 16.9%.

WORLD WAR II (1939–45)

In the run-up to the start of World War II, inflation averaged 2–3% per year, but in 1940 it rose to around 16%, and in 1941 it rose by a further 10%. This lent urgency to a great debate both within and outside government as to how the war should be financed, with John Maynard Keynes playing an important role.

In 1939 *The Times* published three articles by Keynes, and these were subsequently expanded, refined and circulated in a series of notes to the Chancellor of the Exchequer and then published as *How to Pay for the War: A Radical Plan for the Chancellor of the Exchequer*.[6] Keynes believed it was very important to keep the trade union movement on side, and he therefore opposed a straightforward increase in taxes. Instead he recommended introducing tax increases not on gross income but on net income and presenting the increases as a form of forced savings or deferred pay. This was income people could not spend but save by buying National Savings Certificates or Defence Bonds during the course of the war. It was a way for people to increase their net wealth and have funds to draw on when the war finished.

In the 1941 budget prices and rents were fixed at their current level until the end of the war. Because of excess demand at these prices, a system of rationing – involving books of coupons and a points system to ensure fairness – was introduced. To purchase consumption goods, people required two currencies: pounds sterling and ration book points. This proved successful in keeping inflation low. Indeed, there was no measured inflation between 1941 and 1945, which meant that, taken overall from 1939 to 1945, inflation averaged just 7.0%. Then, after two years of high inflation, it averaged only 5%. Capie and Wood estimate that without price controls, and if measured by excess money growth, inflation over the war years would have amounted to 95% – a figure much closer to that experienced during World War I. During most of World War II, as well in the postwar period up until the early 1950s, the true rate of inflation in the United Kingdom was suppressed by rationing.[7]

THE VIETNAM WAR (1964–73)

In the mid 1960s the US president Lyndon B. Johnson decided to escalate the Vietnam War. In 1964 he launched his 'Great Society' welfare programme, which included Medicare and Medicaid and committed the federal government to paying the medical costs of retirees and low-income families. In addition he implemented the first ever Keynesian-inspired tax cut to 'get America moving again' – a move that had first been proposed by President John F. Kennedy.

Soon after this the scale of the war began to escalate, and so too did its costs. By the late 1960s the costs of the war had risen significantly, to the extent that Johnson refused to publish the true estimates of the costs of the war or even disclose them to some of his closest advisers. The budget deficit kept rising, from 0.2% of GDP in 1965 to 2.9% in 1968. Inflation was 0.2% in 1964, but by 1970 it had risen to 5.5%.

The United States was the anchor of the global gold–dollar exchange rate standard that had been established in Bretton Woods in 1944. The dollar was pegged to gold at a price of $35 an ounce and other currencies were fixed at varying prices to the dollar. Countries could revalue or devalue their exchange rates if they found they were consistently at either the top or bottom end of the fixed but adjustable peg. Because of the stresses caused by budget deficits and rising inflation, the United States faced a crucial decision. Under pressure from having to sell gold and repurchase dollars in order to maintain the fixed rate of $35 to an ounce of gold (which was the US commitment under the postwar Bretton Woods international monetary system), President Nixon could have raised interest rates in August 1971. Instead, he decided that the US government was no longer prepared to maintain the convertibility of the dollar. The link between the dollar and gold was cut. Prices then began to rise faster. By 1973 inflation reached 8.7%, and in 1974 it hit 12.3%. Attempts were made to re-establish fixed exchange rates following the breakdown of Bretton Woods, but they were unsuccessful.

The United Kingdom was part of the Bretton Woods international monetary system, with the price of sterling pegged to the US dollar at $2.80 per pound from 1949 but subsequently devalued by the Wilson government to $2.40 to the pound in 1967. As inflation rose in the United States, so too it rose in the United Kingdom: in 1964 retail price inflation was 3.3% but by 1971 it had risen to 9.4%. This increase preceded the Barber Boom of 1972–74, which then increased it by a factor of three to 27%.

THE BARBER BOOM AND THE 1970S INFLATION (1972–82)

The financing of the Vietnam War and the 'Great Society' formed the background to the policies of Harold Wilson's governments. Because of the additional increase in UK government expenditure, the pound was devalued on 18 November 1967, which only added to domestic UK inflationary pressure.

Following the devaluation, Roy Jenkins was appointed Chancellor of the Exchequer, and he pursued a very tight monetary and fiscal policy. Public sector borrowing fell from £1,982 million in 1967–68 to £466 million in the following year. When the Conservative government took office in 1970 it was much the same figure. However, the prime minister, Edward Heath, decided to throw caution to the wind and he boldly aimed for a growth rate of 5% per year for two years in order to ensure success in joining the European Economic

Community (now the European Union) on 1 January 1973. Public sector borrowing increased astronomically: from £804 million in 1970–71 to £1,005 million in 1971–72, £2,532 million in 1972–73 and £4,450 million in 1973–74. Money supply growth followed the same trend: it was low in the late 1960s but then rose to 15% by the autumn of 1971, to 22% by the year end 1971, to 28% by mid 1972 and to just over 25% for the next twelve months. By 1975 inflation had risen to 27.4 % (see figure 2).

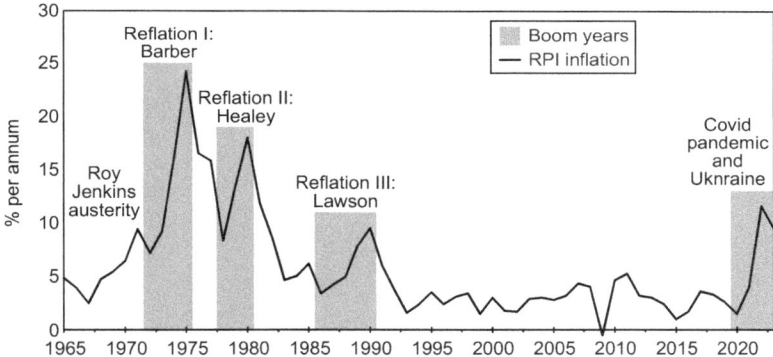

Figure 2. UK retail price inflation (1965–2023). (*Source*: based on datasets published by the Office for National Statistics: 'Consumer price inflation, historical data, UK 1950 to 1988' and 'Consumer price inflation, UK: March 2024'.)

A group of seven economists (Harry Johnson, Alan Walters, Victor Morgan, Malcolm Fisher, S. H. Frankel, David Laidler and myself), an accountant (David Myddelton) and one MP (Richard Body), collectively called the Economic Radicals, co-authored a pamphlet titled 'Memorial to the Prime Minister' that set out the relationship between public borrowing and monetary growth and posed the question:

> Is there another country in the world that can claim a record of such profligacy as that [i.e. the United Kingdom]? It is, we suspect, the clue as to why our rate of inflation is so much worse than that of any other member country of OECD.

The memorial was not well received in 10 Downing Street (see figure 3).

Figure 3. Growth in the net borrowing requirement, from 'Memorial to the Prime Minister' (Economic Radicals, 1974).

COVID INFLATION PREDATES RUSSIA'S WAR IN UKRAINE

The war against Covid is in some ways similar to past military conflicts. Government expenditure in 2020 and 2021 rose spectacularly. The public sector deficit was the largest ever recorded in peacetime. To pay for it, public borrowing rose and the Bank of England increased funding to pay for increased government expenditure through quantitative easing (QE).[8] Taxes were raised: corporation tax, national insurance, a windfall tax on energy companies and the inflation 'stealth tax'. It would have been politically impossible for any government to pay for the war against Covid simply by raising taxes. The result, however, was that, as public sector borrowing exploded, money supply growth rose sharply.

After a lengthy period of building up its military forces on Ukraine's border, Russia invaded Ukraine – a sovereign, independent country – on 24 February 2022. The impact has been a reshaping of the world economic order; the reinvigoration of NATO, with Sweden and Finland joining; and the weaponization of gas and food by President Putin as retaliation for Western countries' supply of arms and economic aid to Ukraine. This has meant that inflation has not been a 'transitory' phenomenon, as central banks claimed: instead, it has risen to over 10% in most Western countries (though not in Japan or Switzerland). In the United Kingdom, inflation reached 11% (consumer price index) and 14% (retail price index) in 2022. Because of the three supply-side shocks – Covid, the Ukraine war and labour force inactivity – public spending rose dramatically.

LESSONS FROM UK WARS

The evidence from the five wars in which the United Kingdom has been involved suggests a common pattern that invariably ends up with inflation either open or suppressed.

- First, when war is declared, a country has one objective: namely, to win. This means the whole economy has to be put on a war footing.

- Second, government expenditures have to increase significantly to obtain equipment and armaments, and to recruit a fighting force to engage the enemy.

- Third, to pay for the war, taxes have to be increased, but typically they cannot be increased sufficiently to pay the total costs of fighting the war.

- Fourth, this means that government borrowing soars, leaving a large overhang of debt to be serviced in peacetime.

- Fifth, the easiest and cheapest method of paying for the war is by printing money (most recently through QE), creating inflation which in effect is a form of taxation, but a form never authorized by parliament.

- Sixth, the cure for inflation is always costly, which is why the years immediately following wars are invariably fraught with difficulty.

In all of the wars in which the UK has been directly involved, it had withdrawn from being on the gold standard, which would otherwise have acted as a form of discipline on government spending and borrowing. The United States left the gold–dollar exchange standard in August 1971 when President Nixon closed the gold window at the Fed, ending convertibility of the dollar into gold at $35 an ounce. If convertibility had been retained, it would have meant higher US interest rates, which would have acted as a constraint on total spending in the United States.

PART II

WHY INFLATION IS A BAD THING

CHAPTER 2

Real economic costs

At the beginning of a period of inflation, far from being perceived as a bad thing, it tends to be welcomed as a good one. Firms enjoy rising prices: revenues increase and governments are lauded by business for pursuing expansionary macroeconomic policies. Typically, the level of interest rates at which people can borrow will have fallen, spending by consumers and businesses will be rising, industrial output will be edging up, companies will be hiring more labour, and the government will feel proud of having cut taxes and increased public spending. Even though the prices of goods and services will not have changed much, the prices of assets such as houses, land, commercial property, equities and more exotic items such as art, wine, jewellery and precious metals will have begun to increase.

It is not long, though, before firms find themselves having to pay more to retain labour and attract staff. Trade unions become resentful because price increases have eroded the purchasing power of the wage increases they previously negotiated. Unsurprisingly, they demand higher wages – not just enough to catch up, but enough to ensure they are not caught out again. As wages – and costs – continue to rise, what might initially have seemed like a good thing becomes clear evidence within twelve months that inflation has taken off.

There is a tendency among economists to belittle the costs of inflation as being far less serious than those relating to unemployment. What really matters, they argue, is the real economy – output, jobs, construction, consumption, capital investment, productivity, the trade balance – not the monetary economy. If the stock of money were to double and all prices, wages, rents, dividends and interest rates also doubled, nothing would have changed because the real economy would not have been affected. People's standard of living would remain unchanged, with the only exception being those who held notes, coins and non-interest-bearing deposits in the bank. In such a world, money is a veil. It is the real economy that provides prosperity and jobs, and it is that which matters, not the money economy.

In his presidential address to the American Economic Association in 1972, the distinguished Yale economist James Tobin, after arguing that the real costs of inflation to a society are trivial (such as the 'shoe-leather costs' of making more frequent visits to the bank in order to hold less cash and the cost to businesses of posting new prices), belittled the real cost of inflation with some humour. According to economic theory, he argued, the real social cost of anticipated inflation is the resources people must use to minimize the amount of non-interest-bearing money, such as currency, that they hold:

> I suspect that intelligent laymen would be utterly astounded if they realized that *this* is the great evil economists are talking about. They have imagined a much more devastating cataclysm, with Vesuvius vengefully punishing the sinners below. Extra trips between [interest-paying] savings banks and [non-interest-paying] commercial banks? What an anti-climax![1]

Tobin makes it clear that he is assuming that inflation is fully anticipated and that everyone is able to make the necessary adjustments. A fully anticipated inflation implies that each person has forecast future inflation correctly, with the result that market prices have responded in such a way that wages, interest rates, the value of savings and government debt, asset prices and so on have all increased to fully reflect the rise in the price level. The only exception is those who lost out because they held money in the form of notes, coins and non-interest-bearing bank deposits.

This distinction between anticipated and unanticipated inflation has the character of an experiment conducted in a university science laboratory – which, of course, it is. That is not to say it is of no use, but it is of limited value when analysing inflation in the real world. Even with unanticipated inflation, economists tend to view it as being primarily a redistribution of income and wealth from savers to debtors rather than as a reduction in income and wealth.

Instead of assuming that inflation is fully expected, a preferable starting point would be the concept of 'radical uncertainty'. This term was coined by Frank Knight, the founder of the Chicago School of Economics, and it has been taken up more recently in the United Kingdom by John Kay and Mervyn King.[2] Risk is when we can measure the impact of a certain event – such as a house fire, a car accident or a flood – and then, on the basis of statistical evidence, assign a probability to it occurring and purchase an insurance policy against it. Radical uncertainty is when it is impossible to do this. It is not a 'known unknown' but an 'unknown unknown'. Many of the major changes in output and prices in recent years have been precipitated by events that it has not been possible to foresee: the fall of the Berlin Wall, China entering the world economy, the Vietnam War, the oil price shocks of 1974 and 1979, the 2008 financial crisis, the US–China trade war, the Covid-19 pandemic, the Russian military invasion of Ukraine, the Hamas terrorist attack against Israel on 7 October 2023, and so on. In a world of radical uncertainty, inflation imposes serious costs on everyone. But how?

First, it diverts real resources from productive use to unproductive use. When the monetary taps are turned on, as they were in 2020 and 2021 in response to Covid, inflation can be expected to rise. However, not enough is known about its likely course to be able to act with confidence. This creates uncertainty for business when it comes to decisions about how often to raise prices and when to invest, or about whether it is necessary to hedge decisions, to anticipate what actions government might take or to negotiate wage increases. If all contracts could be index linked to inflation, inflation's cost to society would be reduced, but the insight of radical uncertainty is that we cannot expect to know any of these things precisely from the limited information we possess during an inflationary process.

The last few years have been a time of radical uncertainty. How rapidly would we see the UK, US and European economies recovering from the Covid contraction? Would consumer spending bounce back, like a coiled spring being released, as vaccinations proceeded apace? Would the Bank of England move to negative interest rates? Would central banks start a process of tapering, selling government bonds into the market rather than buying them from the market? What would happen to the cost of capital? Would the Chancellor of the Exchequer raise taxes and curb expenditure to prevent government debt from soaring to nearly 100%? And if so, how? All these uncertainties posed a challenge for business and investors. Perhaps it would therefore be better to defer investment rather than get it wrong? Maybe a better plan would be to invest in hedges against inflation, such as gold, property, *objets d'art* and collectables, rather than holding cash. These challenges divert resources from investment in productive projects into hedges against inflation.

A second real cost of inflation is that it distorts relative prices, changes in which are a signalling device to indicate either shortages or surpluses of certain goods and services, as well as labour. Because of inflation, individual prices will move to reflect not just shortages and surpluses but also people's expectations of future inflation. This leads to a misallocation of capital and labour, with both being put to less productive use. Prices are a signalling device that allocate resources to their most productive use. During inflation, price rises proceed at different rates in different sectors of the economy, with variable lags between price increases and wage increases. Inflation therefore creates false signals because of the difficulty of distinguishing changes in underlying real prices from those associated with the inflationary process, with the result that capital and labour are allocated by businesses in an inefficient way. Because of uncertainty, inflation forces management to devote more time to figuring out when to raise prices and the way in which competitors will respond. If central banks maintain interest rates at artificially low levels, as they did in the United Kingdom until December 2021, this allows zombie companies to carry on in business, paying interest on their debt so that they can avoid going bust, but at the same time continuing to employ capital and labour that could be more productive in other areas. As such, this represents a further misallocation.

A third real cost of inflation is rising unemployment. In 1958 the London School of Economics professor A. W. Phillips published a paper based on UK empirical data between 1861 and 1967 that showed a historical relationship between unemployment and changes in money wage rates, a relationship often described as the Phillips curve.[3] When unemployment was low, Phillips found wages increased faster as the demand for labour outstripped supply; when unemployment increased, the supply of labour outstripped demand and wage growth slowed. His research was not a theory of inflation but simply a mapping of the historical record. However, in the heyday of short-term Keynesian macroeconomic management, it gave policymakers confidence that such an empirical trade-off existed and that by managing aggregate demand through short-term fiscal policy, there was a menu from which it was possible to achieve a preferred combination of both full employment and price stability.

In the years following World War II, after the removal of rationing and a burst of higher prices, inflation remained low and unemployment averaged less than 2%. From the mid 1960s, though, inflation started to pick up in the United Kingdom, as it did in all major Western economies, but the greatest and most baffling surprise was that, contrary to the relationship described by the Phillips curve, rising inflation became accompanied by rising unemployment. In the 1960s unemployment averaged 2.0% and inflation 3.5%. In the 1970s unemployment averaged 6.4% and inflation 12.6%. The same trend was evident in all major economies bar Germany. With the end of the Bretton Woods system in 1973, the Bundesbank, Germany's central bank, introduced a regime change in its approach to monetary policy by setting targets to control inflation through control of monetary expansion: it introduced simple, transparent and comprehensive targets for the broad monetary aggregates.[4]

The explanation for inflation and unemployment rising together was that workers, in negotiating wage rises, were concerned for the real value of their take-home pay, not just its nominal value. This meant that once inflation had kicked in and become endemic to the economy, a stable, non-accelerating rate of inflation could only be achieved if the labour market settled at a 'natural' rate of unemployment: this is frequently referred to as the non-accelerating inflation rate of unemployment. This rate could be 2%, 5%, 15% or even higher. The important point is that if unemployment were to stay at this rate, it would ensure a stable rate of inflation. In other words, far from being downward sloping, the Phillips curve would, in the long run, be close to vertical at the natural rate of unemployment. The figure for the natural rate would depend on factors such as the bargaining power of trade unions, the cost of acquiring information regarding job vacancies, the cost of geographic mobility, and so on. Charles Goodhart and Manoj Pradhan have estimated that the natural rate of unemployment in advanced economies has varied in recent decades between 2% and 5%. Importantly, it is not fixed: it is constantly shifting due to longer-run demographic, political and economic factors.[5]

A further cost of inflation to society is the cost of bringing it under control. There is no gain without pain. Reducing inflation leads to higher unemployment and lost output. It is excessively painful. To my knowledge there is no evidence so far of any serious inflation having been successfully brought under control without interest rates having been raised significantly, public spending having been cut and/or taxes on persons, households and businesses having been raised. Taken together this inevitably leads to job losses.

When inflation becomes established, and its cost to the economy becomes evident, politicians typically become convinced that they should intervene and introduce some form of price and wage controls. In the 1960s both President John F. Kennedy and Prime Minister Harold Wilson introduced incomes policies through persuasion, 'jaw-boning' or the imposition of statutory ceilings on wages and prices. In its more convincing form, the argument for an incomes policy is that if, when aggregate demand is being reduced, trade unions could be persuaded to modify their wage demands, this would reduce the rise in unemployment that was necessary to reduce inflation.

When I was advising Sir Geoffrey Howe in the period between 1974 and 1979, at the time when he was Margaret Thatcher's shadow Chancellor, he always wished to argue this line, and he kept referring to an article he had published entitled 'Wages policy'. While the logic of the argument I presented in the previous paragraph is correct, in practice incomes policies have invariably led to shortages and provoked trade union militancy, industrial action and strikes – and have subsequently broken down and been abandoned.

When inflation takes off – as it did in the United Kingdom in the 1970s and globally in the immediate aftermath of Covid and before the Ukrainian war – it is never fully anticipated. Inflation imposes a real cost on the economy in terms of reduced output, inefficient allocation of capital and labour, higher unemployment and investment in hedges against inflation.

CHAPTER 3

Heating or eating: the cost of living crisis

The recent inflation was unexpected, and the increase was very large: in 2020 retail price inflation was 1.5%; in 2022 it was 11.6%. For many people it has been a harrowing experience: the price of food (17%), fuel (30%), electricity (65%) and gas (129%) rose astronomically in 2022; rents went up, as did mortgage interest rates; and increases in wages and welfare benefits have not kept pace. There is countless evidence that people have been and are really struggling.

> We are already seeing a huge crisis among the people who are coming to us for help. ... These are real people, like the woman who came to us recently, a single mum who was cut off from gas and electricity. She'd fallen behind on bills after she separated from her partner, she'd been pushed onto a pre-payment meter, she couldn't top it up. ... She's now having to resort to taking her baby's milk to the GP's surgery to warm it up, sitting in her dad's car to keep warm and to charge her phone.[1]

> My partner has recently become sick and as a result I've had to leave work. We've been relying on food banks to get by and been eating smaller portions to make what we have last longer. When my children go into the kitchen to look for food, all I see is the disappointed faces as they find the cupboards empty.[2]

People were suddenly seeing this incredibly precarious situation coming down the track. There was a huge shock as people realised, oh, my God – this is really starting to affect us. Quite early on, we noticed that people were starting to say: it's going to be heat or eat.[3]

There has been much discussion this year about the dilemma people face between 'eating or heating'. From what we've seen at the food bank in recent weeks, we're far beyond that now. Many people can afford to do neither. If you're on a low income and something goes wrong – a benefit sanction or deduction, promised work hours that don't materialise or an urgent, unforeseen expense – you can be left with nothing at all. Forget about eating or heating, you will be starving AND freezing.[4]

THE EMPIRICAL EVIDENCE

Personal responses such as those above are backed up by the available data.

By mid 2022, according to the Office for National Statistics (ONS), almost 90% of adults in the United Kingdom were claiming that their personal cost of living was increasing, with the primary problems being the cost of food, energy and fuel. Over the same period 94% of adults reported that the price of their food shopping had increased, and more than 50% of adults reported spending less on non-essentials and using less energy in their homes. By March 2023 93% of adults said that the cost of living was the most important issue that they were facing, ahead of the NHS (84%), the economy (74%) and climate change and the environment (61%). In July 2023 the ONS stated:

> Around 1 in 20 ... adults reported that in the past two weeks they had ran out of food and had been unable to afford more, this proportion appeared higher among groups including those receiving support from charities (45%), living in a household with one adult and at least one child (28%), receiving some form of benefits or financial support (21%).[5]

This inflation was unexpected and increased rapidly for most households. The monthly average increase in the price of food in March 2020, before the pandemic was declared, was 1.3%. By October 2021 it was still only 1.3%. But in 2022 it started to increase, rising to 9.8% in June of that year, 16.4% in October and 18.2% in February 2023.

The increase in gas prices was even more dramatic. In March 2021 the average level of UK gas prices (sterling) was 1.547 (p/kWh). By March 2022 they had risen to 10.129 (p/kWh). This was partly due to economies opening up after Covid-related lockdowns, but more particularly to Russia's full-scale invasion of Ukraine. By late August 2022 the price had risen above 19 (p/kWh). The effect of these can be seen in figure 4. These prices were free market prices but households throughout these years were partially protected by a price cap and then, from October 2022, by an Energy Price Guarantee, initially for two years.

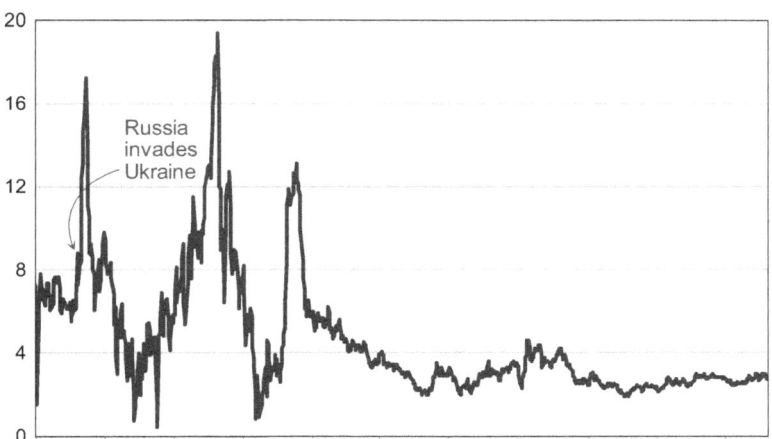

Figure 4. UK wholesale spot price for gas from 2022 onwards (pence per kWh). (*Source*: Paul Bolton, 2024, 'Gas and electricity prices during the "energy crisis" and beyond', House of Commons Library Research Briefing, 2 September. Reproduced under the Open Parliament Licence v3.0.)

A survey conducted by the insurance company Legal & General in March 2023 found that 95% of working households in the United Kingdom had taken a real-terms pay cut over the previous 12 months.[6] For lower-income households the figure was 99%. When asked whether they were concerned about keeping up rent or mortgage payments in the next 12 months, 47% of households said that they were; some people had dipped into short-term savings (27%), tapped into long-term savings (19%), borrowed (14%), stopped making pension contributions (14%) or taken on new credit card debt (14%). For those on low incomes and state benefits, however, the options are more limited: food banks, charities, borrowing from payday lenders. For some the only option was hunger and living in cold temperatures. Only 1% of the poorest households (those with a pretax income of £20,000 or less) received inflation-beating increases, while 33% said their nominal income had fallen.

Citizens Advice records show that the number of people they helped with cost of living issues increased from just over 600,000 in 2020, to 800,000 in 2021, and to nearly 1.1 million in 2022. The increase in those receiving help through the Citizens Advice crisis-support programme was over 200,000 individuals, which was roughly 48% higher than a year earlier. People sought support for a range of issues, relating to energy costs, everyday debts, council tax arrears, prepayment meters, homelessness, benefit entitlements and increasing private rents. The demographic breakdown by household type of those receiving help is interesting: couples made up only 6% of the total, while single persons constituted 35% and single persons with a child or children were highest of all at 40%. Morgan Wild, Citizens Advice head of policy, commented: 'Over the last 12 months we have seen hundreds of thousands of people coming to us for crisis support, many for the first time.'[7]

In May 2022 the New Economics Foundation reported that 2.2 million more people would have to make sacrifices when it came to essentials like putting food on the table or replacing clothes in 2022 than was the case in 2021. The rise in costs for the poorest half of people is nine times larger than for the richest 5% as a proportion of income, and for families in the middle of the income distribution the rise in costs is six times larger.[8] In addition they estimated that

23.5 million people would be unable to afford the cost of living that year. In the following month the Joseph Rowntree Foundation published a survey of the bottom 40% of household earners and found that 60% of that sample had gone without essentials: for example, they had not heated their homes, had cut down on the size of meals, had skipped meals or had gone without basic toiletries.[9]

The increase in the cost of living has hit the lowest-income households disproportionately hard for four reasons.

- First, food, electricity and gas take up a larger proportion of low-income budgets, and those on low incomes tend to live in older houses that are less energy efficient.

- Second, low-income families find it more difficult to cut down on food and heating because doing so damages their health.

- Third, these families tend to have very little savings, and they experience great difficulty trying to obtain credit. When they do manage to do so, it is typically available only if exorbitant charges are paid to money lenders. Also, it is virtually impossible to access increased state welfare benefits.

- Fourth – and this point is frequently neglected – the goods bought by the poorest were more subject to inflationary increases than those used by the most well off: the measure of inflation of goods and services consumed by the poorest third of households was around 12.5%, but for those in the top decile of income it was less, at 9%.

One measure of the seriousness of the cost of living crisis is the way in which it has driven more people to use food banks. A survey of 550 independent food banks in May 2022 found that 93% reported a significant increase in the need for their services, with 95% of those reporting an increase saying it was due to the increased cost of living.[10] More than 70% of food banks also reported a drop in donations over this period. Those most likely to use food banks are social tenants and those with a disability or a health condition, but there is evidence that a wider cross-section of the population has begun to use them, including social workers, public sector workers and teachers. For the clients of Citizens Advice, the number of people being referred to food banks rose significantly, and there were clear demographic differences: during the summer of 2020 the number of single persons with children seeking help was 1,000, and for single persons living alone it was 2,000; during the winter of 2022–23, however, the number grew to 4,000 for the former group and to 5,600 for the latter.

GOVERNMENT SUPPORT

The fact that the rise in inflation was totally unexpected and that people with limited options had no place to turn meant that the government was under great pressure from parliamentarians, commentators and charities to step in and help.

In October 2022 the government introduced a £2,500 Energy Price Guarantee (EPG), capping energy prices and thereby giving one-off support, and it uprated benefits and gave smaller amounts of help to people in special need at a total cost of £94 billion. It also gave households a £400 winter discount to help with energy bills over the 2022–33 winter and provided help to businesses, though not as generously. The cap of £2,500 that was set under the EPG replaced the increase recommended by the energy regulator Ofgem, which would have given a ceiling of £3,549.

The government's approach has been criticized by various think thanks and charities. The National Institute of Economic and Social Research (NIESR) believes the approach was not sufficiently targeted and was therefore unnecessarily expensive. In particular, the poorest households have still found their energy bills increasing. The NIESR would have liked to see energy bills being cut for the poorest – cushioning the impact of the price shock for low- and middle-income households – with the subsidy removed from those who could afford to pay. It proposed a variable energy price cap where the cost of each unit of energy used increases with the level of usage.

The NIESR recognizes that the drawback of their suggestion is that low-income households who are high energy users – because of geography or dependents, or because they live in poorly insulated homes – would be penalized. To remedy this, it suggests introducing additional support packages for this group, including universal credit and general cash payments as a supplement to a variable price cap.[11] By contrast, the Resolution Foundation has emphasised the unequal impact of inflation on poorer and well-off families, with the former losing out, thereby producing an increase in the inequality of income. Its major policy prescription is for the government to target reducing inflation.[12]

RENTS AND MORTGAGES

When prices started to rise sharply in 2022 the squeeze in the cost of living hit low-income families the hardest. Twelve months later – and after fourteen interest rate increases by the Bank of England – younger people, students and mortgagors have begun to feel the impact of rising rents and the increased interest costs of mortgages. Since the pandemic, rents across the United Kingdom have increased by 29%, with young people and students having been particularly badly affected. The supply of rented accommodation has contracted and the supply of council house accommodation has fallen by more than 10% since 2010. Owners of buy-to-let properties are having to refinance their mortgages at much higher rates, which for some makes no commercial sense so they exit the business. This also deters would-be buyers from getting into the business. Reforms introduced by George Osborne during his time as Chancellor of the Exchequer – a 3% stamp duty surcharge on sales of second homes, the abolition of the 10% discount on tax bills for repairs, and the tapering of mortgage interest tax relief – are a disincentive to invest in buy-to-let properties. If tenants fall into arrears, many landlords struggle to pay their increased mortgage payments.

In Scotland, Nicola Sturgeon, former leader of the Scottish National Party and former First Minister, introduced rent controls by freezing rents in social and private housing to protect tenants and address what she called the humanitarian crisis. Since controls were introduced the crisis has got worse, with a reduction in the number of properties available to rent. What is more, the freeze only applied to existing tenancies: those taking out new leases would be subject to new higher rents.

As mortgage costs have risen dramatically, homeowners have been seriously squeezed and some are facing repossession. The Chancellor of the Exchequer has secured a pledge from banks that there will be a twelve-month grace period before repossession proceedings begin. In addition, the Financial Conduct Authority (the sector's regulator) is requiring mortgage providers to extend the length of their mortgage terms and switch to interest-only repayments.

All the evidence – whether it comes from the government, from charities or from the individuals who are worst affected – points to the lowest-income families having suffered most from the current inflation. The government has helped by reducing energy costs and increasing certain benefits, and charities (especially food banks) have risen to the challenge, but for many low-income families the speed at which the prices of food and energy have increased has forced them to the edge – or even into destitution.

CHAPTER 4

Inflation as deceit

Inflation is a given over which people have little control, much like temperature, rainfall, wind and storms. The recent increase in the cost of living has caught most people by surprise and seems to have come out of nowhere. The recent series of supply-side shocks – Covid, the war in Ukraine, the Houthi rebel attacks in the Red Sea – are easily understood, but the role played by central banks is more difficult to understand because it is more technical. Inflation is presented in the media and in parliament, and more generally, in a box labelled 'economics'.

What is missing is that inflation has a moral and ethical dimension that is easily glossed over, and it is this angle that I wish to explore in this chapter.

KEYNES, RÖPKE AND ROBBINS

I have been significantly influenced thinking about inflation by the views of three distinguished academic economists all of whom lived through serious inflations.

We think of John Maynard Keynes as the economist who, at the time of the Great Depression in the 1930s, rescued market capitalism by advocating increased spending by governments not financed by tax increases in order to reduce unemployment. Earlier in his career, however, Keynes lived through inflation averaging 15% annually during World War I, and as the official British representative at the

Paris Peace Conference in 1918–19 worked alongside colleagues from countries who were receiving

> almost hourly the reports of the misery, disorder, and decaying organization of all Central and Eastern Europe, Allied and enemy alike, and learnt from the lips of the financial representatives of Germany and Austria unanswerable evidence of the terrible exhaustion of their countries. ... Paris was a nightmare, and everyone there was morbid. A sense of impending catastrophe overhung the frivolous scene.[1]

When he wrote on the subject of inflation, he pointed out not just the significant economic and social costs of inflation, but also its ethical and moral character. He described it as an 'arbitrary confiscation' by governments of their citizens' wealth and an 'injustice' to those who had saved. In *A Tract on Monetary Reform,* he wrote of 'the evil consequences of instability in the standard of value and its destruction of the psychological equilibrium in society':

> No man of spirit will consent to remain poor if he believes his betters to have gained their goods by lucky gambling. To convert the business man into the profiteer is to strike a blow at capitalism, because it destroys the psychological equilibrium which permits the perpetuance of unequal rewards. The economic doctrine of normal profits, vaguely apprehended by every one, is a necessary condition for the justification of capitalism. The business man is only tolerable so long as his gains can be held to bear some relation to what, roughly and in some sense, his activities have contributed to society.[2]

To offer perspective on the seriousness of inflation Keynes invoked the words of Lenin, whom he claimed had said that 'the best way to destroy the capitalist system was to debauch the currency'. Keynes endorsed this view, stating that 'the process engages all the hidden forces of economic law on the side of destruction and does it in a manner which not one man in a million is able to diagnose'. In another context Keynes asked the question: 'What moral for our present purpose should we draw from this?' His answer: 'We must make it a prime object of deliberate State policy that the standard of value, in terms of which they are expressed, should be kept stable.'[3]

In *The Economic Consequences of the Peace,* Keynes described the way in which he thought inflation would undermine capitalism. Keynes viewed inflation as part of something much greater than just an unfortunate economic failure: for him it was an 'ism', much as capitalism, socialism or communism were 'isms', hence his use of the word 'inflationism'. It was a system of economic disorder, a process of confiscation of the wealth of its citizens by the state, and a denigration of normal business as profiteering. It was effectively legal robbery from their own citizens carried out by governments in secret, unobserved and arbitrary. Because of this it impoverishes many people but is unlike a wealth tax that has legitimacy because it is debated and passed as an Act of Parliament. As an unpredictable tax on the wealth of people, inflation creates a sense of insecurity for people over their planning for the future and in making decisions over how much to save for a rainy day. It destroys confidence in the value of saving and in the purchasing power of the savings people hold. Frequently neglected is the fact that it undermines the middle classes, which are typically the bedrock of a society and the custodians of bourgeois virtues.

Wilhelm Röpke was very different from Keynes in his social and political philosophy. He was an economics professor at the University of Marburg in the 1930s but was forced to resign his position when the Nazis came to power in Germany. He had witnessed the devastation of inflation in Germany in 1923 and later argued in *A Humane Economy: The Social Framework of the Free Market* that 'the chronic inflation of our age is a moral and social problem'[4] and that 'inflation is not just a disorder of the monetary system which can be left to financial experts to address, it is a moral disease, a disorder of society'.[5] He observed that people wished to invest more than saving allowed, claim wages higher than the rise in productivity, consume more than current income could justify, import more goods than were exported, and allow the government to spend more than it received in tax revenue. Inflation is a continuous strain on our resources: 'The trouble is that we lack counterforces of a spiritual, moral and social nature. In the realm of ideas we no longer have definitive convictions and guiding principles.'[6]

In 1972 inflation was taking off in the United Kingdom. It would eventually reach 27%, but long before it did, Lord Robbins, who had built up the economics department at the London School of Economics as a rival to that at the University of Cambridge, concluded his opening remarks as chairman of a conference on inflation in the same year with the following words:

> I would attack inflation not merely because of the effects on production and distribution but also because of the effects on general morale. One has no idea, unless one has lived at some time in a country inflating at a brisk rate, or unless one is alive to what is happening here, of the subtle effects it has on private or public honesty and eventually on the political solidarity of the society in which it takes place. I would not wish to falsify history by oversimplification: but anyone who wishes to understand the reason why the Nazis, with all the appalling nonsense they preached, managed to secure so much passive adherence among the more sober-minded citizens of their country must realise that standards of public morals, standards of public decency, expectations of possibilities, had been sapped in various ways by inflation. ... Democracy certainly stands to be undermined by inflation and what is even more fundamental, the free society itself.[7]

As can be seen from the words used to describe inflation by these three distinguished academics – 'disorder', 'decay', 'arbitrary confiscation', 'ethical and moral character', 'injustice', 'evil consequences', 'moral problems', 'moral disease', 'disorder of society', 'spiritual counterforces', 'public and private honesty', 'public morals', 'public decency', 'political solidarity' – inflation most definitely has a moral and ethical dimension.

The current inflation has demonstrated once again the painful costs it imposes on people. We tend to think of inflation in terms of two separate categories: single-figure inflation, which can be managed, and hyperinflation, such as that seen in 1923 in Germany and more recently in Zimbabwe and Venezuela. We assume that single-figure inflation is something 'transitory' – it can be brought under control with difficulty, but it is manageable. However, once inflation takes off, it is far from easy to stabilize at a higher rate: it can be volatile and mutate into stagflation, or it can escalate into hyperinflation. The lesson to take away is that rapid inflation and hyperinflation *both* start with moderately rising inflation that governments think they can manage.

INFLATION AS A FORM OF DECEIT

According to the Oxford English Dictionary deceit is a 'concealment of the truth in order to mislead; deception, fraud, cheating'. To issue banknotes when inflation is firmly expected to continue above its target rate is a form of deceit.

We live in an economy in which money plays a critical role. The importance of money derives from the fact that those who hold it trust that others will accept it as a means of payment. Without stable money we would be forced to return to some form of barter. A stable currency is the basis for trust in business, trust in saving and investing, trust in government and trust in the future of democracy. Otmar Issing was a member of the board of Deutsche Bundesbank and a distinguished professor of economics before he played a key role in the establishment of the euro and became a member of the executive board of the European Central Bank. He wrote that: 'Trust in stable money is also the basis for a free society, the ability of people to take decisions and plan their future for themselves.'[8] Stable money is key to prosperity. When, because of inflation, stability is undermined, confidence in the economy will be undermined and so will the trustworthiness of central banks and government Treasuries.

In earlier societies the transition to a money economy was based on something with intrinsic value: that is, something that has value independent of its use as money. Metal coins were developed as money and stamped with an official mark to certify their weight. The British pound takes its name from the Latin *pondus*, meaning weight. 'Sterlings' were silver coins issued in Anglo Saxon times. A shekel was a silver coin and a measure of weight; the word is derived from *siglu*, a root expressing the action of weighing.

Rulers who were desperate to fund wars and buy peace either clipped coins or reminted them using less valuable metals. History records that countries in the ancient Near East – such as those in Babylonia during Persian rule in the third millennium BCE and in Egypt during the later second millennium BCE – experienced periods of serious inflation.[9] However, the practice of devaluing the coinage was condemned as dishonest. In the Old Testament this was made absolutely clear: 'Do not use dishonest standards when measuring length, weight, or quality. Use honest scales and honest weights' (Leviticus: 19:35–36). To tamper with weights and measures was not just an illegal act but an offence against almighty God: 'The Lord abhors dishonest scales, but accurate weights are his delight' (Proverbs 11:1). Around the time the book of Isaiah was written (circa 700 BCE), unethical silversmiths who debased the currency were condemned: 'Your silver has become dross, your wine mixed with water' (Isaiah 1:22). Debasing the coinage was a moral failure.

Historically, what was printed on the face of an English banknote was the promise to receive physical gold in exchange for the promissory note. Throughout most of the nineteenth century the price of a pound sterling was fixed at $20.65 per ounce of gold. During the Great Depression it was revalued to $35 per ounce. The Bretton Woods international financial system established after World War II still had gold at the anchor of the system. The dollar was fixed in price to gold at $35 per ounce and the US government agreed to buy and sell gold at that price. The US government decided to end the link with gold in 1971 and the gold–dollar exchange standard was replaced by flexible exchange rates. Today, our currency is not a commodity-based money but a 'fiat' money, from the Latin for 'let it be done'. The government simply announces that certain coins and banknotes (formerly paper, now polymer) are legal tender, meaning they will be recognized by law as a means to make payments. Fiat money has little intrinsic value. It is because of the authority of government that notes and coins have a face value above their intrinsic value, which in turn has the backing of courts of law. In other words, fiat money is based on the public's faith in the issuer of the currency: namely, the Bank of England and, standing behind the central bank, and with the ability to raise taxation and borrow to finance expenditure, His Majesty's Treasury.

Today, this commitment to stability is the 2% target rate of inflation. The target is set by the Chancellor of the Exchequer, and if it is missed the governor of the Bank of England is required to write to the Chancellor and explain why. A failure to achieve the target is effectively a broken promise.

The commitment on the face of all Bank of England notes is very clear. For example, on a £20 note it says 'I promise to pay the bearer on demand the sum of twenty pounds', and that promise is signed by the chief cashier of the Bank of England. If in one year's time its value is only eighteen pounds, that represents a broken promise. A banknote is more than a means of payment or a store of value: it also has a symbolic quality. The chief cashier's signature represents the tradition and values of the nation. When the chief cashier's signature first appeared on banknotes in 1870, people took pride in the fact that the pound sterling stood for honesty, prudence and price stability and that it was the major currency in which world trade was conducted. US Federal Reserve dollar bills have the words 'In God We Trust' on them, seemingly invoking the Almighty to preserve the value of the currency. This first appeared in 1960 when the dollar had replaced sterling as the world's leading currency, once again standing for freedom, constitutional democracy and prosperity. Euro banknotes make no such promises.[10]

Professor Herbert Frankel has argued that the conception of money that we have inherited historically was about much more than something accepted by the public and the government in settlements of debts. According to Frankel, money was 'a mark of the character of society: the degree of its certainty, dependability and credibility'. He went on 'men should regard money as above suspicion because they realised that it could, finally, only reflect what society was.'[11] Ultimately, the keeping of promises and the discharging of obligations involves only one essential principle: 'Morality in the free monetary order is indivisible.'[12]

THE INFLATION TAX

Inflation is not only deceit, it is a form of taxation. It is as much a tax as VAT, petrol duty or inheritance tax. As Keynes wrote: 'What is raised by printing notes is just as much taken from the public as is a beer-duty or an income tax. What a Government spends the public pays for. There is no such thing as an uncovered deficit.'[13] What is more, it is a 'stealth tax'; it is more analogous to a theft or a robbery, but with specious legality because it is undertaken with the sanction of government. The largest single beneficiary of the tax is the government itself. Any tax imposed by government is a way of reducing the spending power of the general public while enabling the government to increase real resources for its own use and at virtually zero cost. As Keynes was keen to point out, inflation is not just the confiscation of wealth by the government, it is an *arbitrary* confiscation. It is capricious and unpredictable. It is guided more by circumstances than by any thought-out policy.

Typically, debtors benefit from inflation and creditors lose out. Those holding cash or non-indexed bonds and those providing mortgages will find that the real value of their assets has fallen. Those issuing cash and bonds and those holding fixed-rate mortgages will find that the real value of their wealth has risen. Those in retirement and especially the professional middle class – teachers, doctors, academics, scientists, researchers and, in the past, lawyers and accountants – lose out, while entrepreneurs, traders in financial markets and those holding real assets such as houses benefit.

Inflation acts as a tax in three ways.

First, it is a tax on the holding of money balances: notes and coins held by the general public. If I hold a £20 note for one year and the rate of inflation is 10%, then the purchasing power of my note in one year's time will be 10% less than it is now: i.e. £18.

Second, the government benefits from inflation by paying off its debts with pounds that have a lower value than when the funds were originally borrowed. During the 1970s, UK inflation was far higher than could have been expected in, say, 1970. The yield on a 10-year gilt-edged stock in that year was 8.5%. Consider a person who bought a bond when it was issued and reinvested the annual coupon. They could expect to earn a cumulative return of nearly 130%: significantly more than doubling their money in nominal terms. Even if we assume they expected inflation throughout the 1970s to be what it averaged in the second half of the 1960s, they would still have expected a total real return (allowing for inflation) of more than 50%. During the 1970s inflation actually averaged 13% per year though, yielding a real return to investors of *minus* 35%. Thus, that inflation allowed the government to pay back their borrowing with money, the value of which was significantly less than that which they received when they issued the bonds.[14]

Third, inflation is a tax through 'fiscal drag'. This occurs when the government does not increase tax thresholds and tax allowances to keep up with inflation or wage growth, so that more of a taxpayer's income is taxable and more taxpayers are dragged into paying tax at higher rates. In the Spring Budget 2021, the Chancellor (Rishi Sunak) announced that the threshold would be uprated for 2021/22 and then frozen until 2026. In the Autumn Statement later that year, he announced that the freeze would be extended to 2028 instead of 2026. This freeze will raise more than £25 billion in tax per year in 2027/28. The move has considerably increased the number of income tax payers who pay tax at the higher rate of 40%: three decades ago the number was one in twenty taxpayers; soon it will be one in five.

Inflation indirectly raises government revenue by automatically moving income tax payers into higher tax brackets, with the government failing to increase allowances or tax credits in line with inflation. In the case of companies, the same thing happens if the government fails to increase the depreciation allowance in line with inflation.

In effectively reducing the value of the currency in order to enable the government to meet its debt obligations, inflation transfers wealth from citizens and businesses to the state. It is therefore a form of taxation – and a discreditable one at that. It is a tax that is not debated by MPs nor passed by an Act of Parliament, and as such it lacks democratic legitimacy. No authorities in the field of taxation would ever recommend it as a way of raising revenue for government. It imposes a tax burden that serves no social or redistributive purpose. It is simply a way for governments to raise funds for activities they could not otherwise undertake. Unlike other forms of theft, there is no requirement to demonstrate a *mens rea* (guilty mind) on the part of ministers, civil servants or other public servants responsible for inflation.

From a government point of view the beauty of an inflation tax is that it is widely spread, costs very little to collect and cannot be avoided. It has typically been used in a dramatic way to finance wars and by profligate governments that do not have the support of their citizens and that are therefore unable to finance their expenditure through taxation or borrowing, and so have to resort to printing money or, today, expanding the money supply through digital means.

Inflation is more than an economic issue. It has a moral and an ethical dimension. It is at heart a form of deceit. Inflation is a discreditable form of taxation – one that restricts the spending power of households, businesses and charities in order for the government to increase its expenditure.

CHAPTER 5

A culture of distrust

Trust is an important element in generating and maintaining economic prosperity. We need to explore how inflation undermines trust in money and in turn creates a culture of distrust that undermines both the trustworthiness of central banks and economic prosperity.

In the 1950s Edward C. Banfield, a professor of political science at the University of Chicago (and subsequently Harvard), was living with his wife and children in a rural community in Portenza in Southern Italy. He was conducting research into the cause of the region's desperate poverty and he gave the town in the region in which he was living a fictitious name: Montegrano. Not only was the town desperately poor, but it also had few political structures, no organized charities or volunteers, no sources of commercial credit and it lacked public-spiritedness. The community consisted of strong self-interested 'families' who cared only for the interests of their 'family'. The family was the only source of social security. They were distrustful of other 'families', whom they viewed as competitors, even enemies, who would attack them if they could; so they must be prepared to respond in kind.[1]

On the basis of his research, Banfield concluded that the poverty of Montegrano was not rooted in the class structure of its society or in the lack of economic planning by the state, but in a culture of distrust, envy and suspicion. The people of Montegrano were prisoners of their family-centred ethos. The fundamental problem was a lack of trust. The beliefs, values and associations that enabled individuals to act not just for themselves but for the good of others was lacking. For Montegrano, a lack of trust in other families and in the social and economic life of the communities in which they lived was the root of its poverty. They had no concept of the public interest or the common good.

Similarly, if the financial crisis of 2008 has only one lesson to teach us, it is the importance of trust in financial markets. In the years before the crisis there was growing criticism of banks and bankers because of reckless financial risk taking, compensation levels that were seemingly unrelated to real wealth creation and ostentatious greed. As John McFall, the chair of the House of Commons Treasury Committee, remarked, the City of London was perceived as an island in the North Sea, some way off the United Kingdom.

At the height of the banking crisis in October 2008, trust between banks collapsed. The UK Parliamentary Commission on Banking that investigated the crisis concluded that it was a 'collapse of trust on an industrial scale'. Banks refused to lend overnight to other banks because they feared they might be insolvent. Short-term financial markets dried up, and with them so did liquidity. Without government intervention, banks would have been forced to close their doors and ATMs would have been left empty. The most serious long-term damage from the financial crisis has been the loss of trust in banks by central banks, investors, politicians, regulators and the general public. As the financial crisis unravelled, every aspect of banking on which the public based their trust was undermined.

Much as a flourishing financial system needs to be based on trust, so does a society and its economy. By creating a culture of distrust, inflation has a subtle but detrimental impact on the culture of a society and the success of its economy. Inflation forces people to think about the higher prices they are being charged. This creates a suspicion that other people are doing them down. There is a sense that because of inflation everyone is on the make, using collusion and a lack of candour to exploit consumers. In late March 2022, BT, EE, Plusnet, TalkTalk and Vodafone (the leading five firms in UK communications) all increased their prices on the same day by more than 9% even though CPI was only 6%. According to Oliver Shah, the price of Pret A Manger's filter coffee had recently increased by no less than 50%.² Brooke Masters reported that companies were changing product size, providing less for the same price: bags of Doritos contained fewer chips, Unilever's Dove body wash dropped from 22 ounces to 20 ounces, and Cottonelle toilet rolls had lost twenty-eight sheets.³

This culture of distrust is not a purely recent phenomenon and was captured brilliantly by Margaret Drabble in her 1970s novel *The Ice Age* (1977):

> Over the country depression lay like fog, which was just about all that was missing to lower spirits even further, and there was even a little of that in East Anglia. All over the nation, families who had listened to the news looked at one another and said 'Goodness me' or 'Whatever next' or 'I will give up' or 'Well, fuck that', before embarking on an evening's viewing of colour television, or a large hot meal, or a trip to the pub, or a choral society evening. All over the country people blamed other people for the things that were going wrong – the trades unions, the government, the miners, the car workers, the seamen, the Arabs, the Irish, their own husbands, their own wives, their own idle good-for-nothing offspring, comprehensive education. Nobody knew whose fault it really was but most people managed to complain fairly forcefully about somebody: only a few were stunned into honourable silence.⁴

The blame culture that Margaret Drabble expresses here has a remarkably contemporary ring to it: gas companies, oil majors, Putin, rail unions, teachers, supermarkets, landlords, restaurants, nurses, consultant doctors, junior doctors, civil servants, the Houthis. All have been blamed for the recent squeeze on the cost of living.

As inflation rises it creates a culture of 'profiteering' that is hugely resented, especially by the professional classes working in the public sector. Inflation is viewed as creating opportunities for speculation by buying properties to rent rather than occupy and investing in assets, such as gold, crypto and *objets d'art*.

Within the public sector it is the government that is blamed. An unprecedented increase in industrial action has led to strikes and threatened strikes by ambulance workers, university lecturers, rail workers, London Underground drivers, airport staff, school teachers, civil servants, barristers, the Border Force, bus drivers, security guards, firefighters and Driving and Vehicle Licensing Agency (DVLA) staff. In the summer of 2022, some trade union leaders in the rail industry threatened to call a general strike of all public sector workers. A total of 2.7 million days were lost in strikes between June and December 2022. For comparison, the total days lost to strikes in the five years between 2015 and 2019 was 1,255: an average of 250 per year.

Inflation leads to distrust in institutions. The Bank of England, the Federal Reserve and the European Central Bank all initially insisted in 2021 that the rise in inflation was 'transitory' and would soon return to the target 2%. As inflation rose to more than five times its official target, the central banks recognized that they had miscalculated. Inflation was far from 'transitory'. As policy veered off course in the United Kingdom, the credibility of both the Bank of England and the Treasury in conducting monetary and fiscal policy was undermined. By June 2023 it was clear that confidence in the Bank had taken a major hit because of its failure to control inflation.[5]

TRUST AND MONEY

Trust is having confidence that other people will tell the truth and keep their promises. Trust means one can believe what other people say without checking the facts. One can rely on other people's promises without demanding guarantees. Trust is the basis of relationships and the glue that binds a community together. Trust is laborious to build, but easy to destroy. Trust is based on truth, and truth is objective, not subjective. Trust is about facts, not opinions. Trust can never simply be expressed as 'my truth', 'your truth', 'their truth'. The people of Southern Italy whom Banfield studied had decided how other families intended to act and did not trust their promises. Following the 2008 financial crisis people did not trust banks. In any kind of transaction, trust saves both time and cost.

Trust depends on trustworthiness. If a business, a central bank or a government wishes to be trusted, it must be trustworthy. It must be relied upon to be honest and truthful in its dealings with its customers, its clients, regulators and the general public. It must be open and transparent about the services it provides and the prices it charges. It must recognize it has a fiduciary responsibility to those it serves. If public sector bodies are to be trusted, they must be considered trustworthy in the same way. They must be competent, honest and reliable. Otmar Issing recognized this:

> Money represents a promise. It requires trust on the part of the users of money that the issuer of money will honour this promise. Money is built on trust but in turn must be built on solid foundations. The promise must be made credible and this – at least in relatively modern times – is the job of central bankers.[6]

Money performs an important function in society. It acts as a medium of exchange. It enables us as individuals to buy and sell goods and services without having to resort to barter. It oils the wheels of commerce and trade. It provides a vehicle for people to save in a readily available form. Money has developed in very different societies precisely because it is a means of exchange, even if what has counted as money has varied enormously: from cowrie shells to gold, paper, bank deposits and (more recently, and only to a limited extent) crypto currencies.

For people to treat coins, notes and bank deposits as money, they must have confidence that they will be accepted by the other party as a means of payment. It is not critical that banknotes are issued by state-owned institutions. What matters is that the public has trust in the issuing institution, and if that institution is a central bank that controls the supply of banknotes, people need to trust that the central bank is competent, reliable and transparent.

While money today – unlike in the nineteenth-century gold standard period – is not exactly a 'fiction', according to Charles Goodhart it is 'a sight liability of the government'. People expect that they can use Bank of England notes to make a payment and in return are prepared to accept notes as change. What is needed, therefore, is trust that the government will honour that liability. During a war or a civil war, when a government is overturned, its money issue typically becomes worthless – as happened under the Confederacy during the American Civil War and in Germany in 1923.

By contrast, a debit or credit card is not money: it is simply evidence that a person has either money or, at least in principle, access to it. When a payment is made using a debit card, the payer's deposit in the bank's balance sheet will be reduced and the payee's account will be credited. In the United Kingdom the major source of money to settle transactions is not notes and coins but bank deposits at commercial banks that have accounts at the Bank of England.

The Bank of England is a public body in law and part of the executive arm of the government. It is independent of the Treasury by Act of Parliament, but it must nevertheless accept instructions from it. Because of this, the Bank of England's credibility rests on the credibility of the Treasury and the UK government. The economic credibility of the government depends in turn on whether it can finance its expenditures by taxation or borrowing. It can borrow on the capital markets, but only at a price. If investors begin to believe that it might not be able to service or redeem its debt because it cannot raise sufficient tax revenue, the interest paid on its debt (gilt-edged securities) will rise, investors will lose confidence in the pound sterling, and – if the currency fails – the government will be unable to raise funds and might be forced to default. In the nineteenth century, when UK governments were unable to raise taxes to finance expenditure, they had to resort to printing more banknotes. Britain did this during the Revolutionary Wars against France and did so again in the twentieth century during World War I. In the 1960s and 1970s when the UK government was in financial difficulty the only option left open to it short of default was for it to go cap in hand to the International Monetary Fund.

TRUST BUT VERIFY

The Russian proverb 'trust but verify' was one that President Ronald Reagan used in connection with disarmament negotiations with the Soviet Union. But does trust have to be verified? At first sight it seems like an oxymoron. The whole point of trust is that it does not have to be verified. Having to constantly verify trust is a seeming contradiction. On the other hand, not doing any verification at all leaves one open to the charge of blind trust and of being imprudent.

In her 2004 Reith Lectures, Baroness Onora O'Neill – a University of Cambridge philosopher and cross-bench member of the House of Lords – argued that:

> We place and refuse trust, not because we have torrents of information, but because we can trace *specific* bits of information and *specific* undertakings to *particular* sources on whose veracity and reliability we can run some tests. *Well-placed trust grows out of active inquiry rather than blind acceptance.*[7] [Emphasis added.]

In the same way, a lack of trust can be traced to specific information, a prior experience, the judgement of a trusted friend. The injunction to verify is not a lack of trust: it is simply prudence.

Money creation by a central bank during a period of inflation raises questions of ethics and morality. If a central bank creates new money that commercial banks are required to hold and that the general public need for everyday transactions, and if it does so at a time when inflation is continuing apace, is it open to the charge of being dishonest? Is the central bank setting a standard for the economy as a whole that is fundamentally unethical? Does it give public servants or politicians any right to challenge the ethics of profiteers, hoarders or people buying and selling on black markets? Does it undermine the trustworthiness of a central bank? Are the monetary authorities setting a standard for economic life that lacks integrity?

In summary, any effective, modern, functioning economy requires trust in money if it is to function properly. Money is, however, essentially a fiction. It can only be effective if the public has confidence in its value. Inflation destroys the value of money and with it trust in money as a means of exchange and a store of value. This in turn raises important questions regarding the trustworthiness of central banks and Treasuries and their ability to ensure confidence in the medium-term prospects for the overall economy to generate economic growth and tax revenue.

CHAPTER 6

'Things fall apart'

After a period as a reforming Home Secretary in the mid 1960s, Roy Jenkins was appointed Chancellor of the Exchequer in 1967. One of his first jobs was to introduce austerity measures following the United Kingdom's devaluation of the pound. His father had worked as a coalminer before becoming a Labour Member of Parliament, which made his decisions as Chancellor doubly painful. After a period out of office, he later became Home Secretary and deputy leader of the Labour Party but resigned as an MP in 1976 in order to become the president of the European Commission.

In November 1979 Jenkins delivered the prestigious Richard Dimbleby Lecture on the BBC. He gave his lecture the title 'Home Thoughts from Abroad' – the words taken from a poem by Robert Browning. By this time Jenkins had become an establishment figure, described by one journalist as 'slightly semi-detached ... an aristocratic egghead ... a sleek and self-consciously sophisticated lover of croquet, tennis, fine wines and aristocratic women ... a most improbable leader of a workers' party'.[1]

He concluded his lecture with words from a poem by W. B. Yeats, the Nobel Prize winning Irish poet, entitled *The Second Coming*:

> The best lack all conviction, while the worst
> Are full of passionate intensity.
> Things fall apart, the centre cannot hold.

The poem uses the metaphor of falconry to illuminate the uncertain future state of the world. The falcon becomes separated from the falconer and, rising higher and higher in the sky, spiralling upward in ever-widening gyrations, the end is captured in the memorable line: 'Things fall apart, the centre cannot hold.'
Things fall apart because the relationship between the falcon and the falconer has been broken. Similarly, anarchy, violence and bloodshed seem to be everywhere. The forces that bring order have collapsed and there is a terrifying sense of disintegration and chaos. Yeats wrote the poem in 1919 following the inflations and hyperinflations of devastated countries following World War I, the Russian Revolution and the Irish struggle for independence. Somewhat hubristically we tend to imagine that such disasters cannot occur in the United Kingdom or other G7 countries. However, the events of the 1970s suggest that there is a danger in overconfidence because of our history.

THE THREE-DAY WEEK (1973–74)

Before leaving UK politics for Brussels, Jenkins experienced the devastating effect of inflation following the breakdown of Edward Heath's incomes policy and the imposition of a compulsory three-day week for all UK firms, resulting in a general election fought over the question: 'Who Governs Britain?'

Some background is necessary here.

The key to British economic policy in the post-war years was consensus. The Wilson governments of 1964–70 and 1974–76, the Heath government of 1970–74 and the Callaghan government of 1976–79 all adhered to the tenets of 'Butskellism'. The name derives from Rab Butler (Conservative Chancellor of the Exchequer in 1954/55) and Hugh Gaitskell (his Labour predecessor in 1950/51), who championed it in the 1950s. They and the governments of the time believed in a mixed economy consisting of private and public sectors with considerable state ownership of large tracts of the economy. When inflation became a serious challenge in the late 1960s and throughout the 1970s, all governments attempted to broker deals between business and trade unions. Voluntary norms were set for wage and price ceilings. These arbitrary norms were invariably exceeded and then became statutory. Extensive research suggested that, at first, prices and incomes policy seemed to offer some success, but all such policies eventually failed because of the complexity of such deals, involving a myriad of different local markets and the inconsistency between the arbitrary norms and the strength of monetary and fiscal policy. Despite the repeated failures of Butskellist income policies, governments made an enormous effort to make them succeed.

The year 1973 was difficult for the government. Inflation had risen from 7% to 10%, the price of a barrel of oil had surged from $2.40 to $11.65, the trade deficit was at a record high, coal production had fallen, and in November the government declared its fifth state of emergency in three years. Sir Douglas Allen, Permanent Secretary to the Treasury, talked of 'the possibility of our moving into a siege economy with rationing on the wartime model'[2] and the sociology professor Oliver McGregor suggested that 'political democracy will not survive in Britain'.[3] The Cabinet Secretary Sir John Hunt commented later: 'It struck me that the smell of death was around.'[4] Geoffrey Rippon, Secretary of State for the Environment, was reported to have said at a private dinner party that Britain was 'on the same course as the Weimar governments, with runaway inflation and high unemployment at the end'.[5]

Then, on 1 January 1974, the three-day week was imposed. This restricted the use of electricity by factories and businesses to three days per week. As Dominic Sandbrook put it in his book *State of Emergency, Britain 1970–74*:

> Nothing like it had ever been seen before in Britain in peacetime, and life during the last days of 1973 had a faint, domesticated whiff of the last days of Pompeii about it, with reports of people queueing outside the shops for bread, candles, paraffin, toilet paper and cans of soup.[6]

Anthony Barber, the Chancellor of the Exchequer, told the House of Commons:

> The issue at stake is whether our affairs are to be governed by the rule of reason, by the rule of Parliament ... and democracy or (by) ... chaos, anarchy and a totalitarian or communist regime.[7]

Although he was not by now a member of the Shadow Cabinet because of his advocacy of closer integration with the European cause, Roy Jenkins insisted that the government was right not to give in to the miners, who were on strike demanding higher pay, because 'if we did, we would soon have domestic inflation of 25% or more'. Inflation subsequently rose to 27%.

Margaret Drabble again captured the mood of the public:

> The old headline phrases of freeze and squeeze had for the first time become for everyone – not merely for the old and unemployed – a living image, a reality: millions who had groaned over them in steadily increasing prosperity were now obliged to think again. A huge icy fist, with large cold fingers, was squeezing and chilling the people of Britain, that great and puissant nation, slowing down their blood, locking them into immobility, fixing them in a solid stasis, like fish in a frozen river: there they all were in their large houses and their small houses, with their first mortgages and second mortgages, in their rented flats and council flats and basement bedsits and their caravans: stuck, congealed, amongst possessions, in attitudes, in achievements they had hoped next month to shed, and with which they were now condemned to live. The flow had ceased to flow: the ball had stopped rolling: the game of musical chairs was over. *Rien ne va plu*s, the croupier had shouted.[8]

The increasing divergence between the falcon and the falconer – the public and the government – is a gradual progression. It takes off with an unexpected surge in public spending followed by an unexpected increase in money supply growth, then rising prices, a cost of living crisis, workers feeling cheated by the reduction in the purchasing power of their wages, bitter disputes – especially in the public sector – leading to industrial action and strikes, accompanied by a loss of confidence in the government to govern. The falcon cannot hear the falconer, and this eventually leads to the downfall of the government itself: 'Mere anarchy is loosed upon the world.'

The distinguished historian Professor Lord Kenneth Morgan wrote that 'the social conflict in industry, certainly, was on a scale and of a character not seen since the days of the Triple Alliance, Black Friday and the General Strike between 1919 and 1926'. At times during 1973 and early 1974 there were daily violent confrontations. As Lord Morgan concluded: 'It would be absurd to deny that something very unusual and alarming was taking place... A sense of potential civil war loomed in England's green but no longer pleasant land.'[9]

At the same time as this was happening there were rumours of private anti-union groups being prepared to launch a coup led by the eccentric extremists Colonel Stirling and General Walker. Newspapers were full of stories of 'Colonel Blimp' and the 'Phantom Major'.[10]

Looking back almost fifty years, it is still hard to believe what actually took place. In 1974 General Sir Walter Walker, a highly respected soldier who had held very senior office in NATO, set up a strike-breaking organization called Unison and began recruiting thousands of people to take over vital services if a general strike was called. The following year Colonel David Stirling set up the Great Britain 1975 Organisation (GB75). Both men had impressive military careers. Walker was a retired general in the British Army and Stirling had founded the Special Air Service (SAS) in 1941 and then led it until 1943. They both distrusted Harold Wilson's government and knew that the government feared a general strike. They also distrusted Edward Heath, the former prime minister, because he had 'surrendered' to the miners. They knew from friends that there was no evidence of continuity planning in the armed forces and no evidence of the regular or territorial army being prepared. However, they feared that a general strike would lead to the closure of power-generating plants and that this would seriously damage morale.

GB75 was established not to launch a *coup d'etat* but to raise a volunteer force to cope with the immediate crisis that would follow the announcement of a general strike. David Stirling made it very clear that it would 'await a formal request from the government before intervening in a major political strike situation and would not thus be acting outside the law'.[11] Stirling and Walker received enormous publicity – and they claimed that the response from the public to this publicity was equally enormous.

In early 1974, when the National Union of Mineworkers voted to strike for the second time, the political situation became what can only be described as anarchy. The prime minister had declared a three-day working week to economize on power supplies, the streets were dark at night, restaurants were lit by candles, and public service television was only available for a limited number of days per week. This led to an election being called by the prime minister over 'who governs Britain'. I was a candidate in said election, defending the government: my first entry into politics.

THE WINTER OF DISCONTENT 1978–79

Roy Jenkins gave his Richard Dimbleby Lecture in November 1979, six months after the Labour government had been voted out of office. The reason Jenkins referred in the lecture to the lines from Yeats's poem – 'Things fall apart; the centre cannot hold' – was because of the disastrous Winter of Discontent* between the autumn of 1978 and the spring of 1979 when there were major strikes. Domestic rubbish was not collected, so it piled up on the streets; schools closed because of a strike by school caretakers; and, in Liverpool and part of Manchester, a strike by gravediggers and crematorium workers led to bodies being stored at a factory and burial at sea being considered as an option. On 22 January 1979, 1.5 million public service workers did not show up for work. Between November 1978 and February 1979, 7.85 million working days were lost to strikes – some official but many unofficial, random, uncoordinated and local.

'THINGS FALL APART; THE CENTRE CANNOT HOLD'

Inflation is an insidious cancer in a liberal democratic society. What starts as an act of deceit creates a culture of distrust, leading to strikes and social conflict and putting strain on a parliamentary democracy to hold together. The inflation of 1972–75, which reached 27%,

---

* The expression Winter of Discontent was an allusion to the well-known quotation from Shakespeare's play Richard III and originally used in *The Sun* newspaper on 3 May 1979.

destroyed people's savings, rewarded speculators and undermined the middle class.

When Keynes reflected on the consequences of the Great War (1914–18) and the inflation – and, in some countries, hyperinflations – that accompanied and followed, he wrote:

> There may, therefore, be ahead of us a long, silent process of semi-starvation, and of a gradual, steady lowering of the standards of life and comfort. The bankruptcy and decay of Europe, if we allow it to proceed, will affect every one in the long-run, but perhaps not in a way that is striking or immediate.
>
> In this autumn of 1919, in which I write, we are at the dead season of our fortunes. The reaction from the exertions, the fears, and the suffering of the past five years is at its height. Our power of feeling or caring beyond the immediate questions of our own material well-being is temporary eclipsed… We have been moved beyond endurance, and need rest. Never in the lifetime of men now living has the universal element in the soul of man burnt so dimly.[12]

'THE SECOND COMING' BY W. B. YEATS (1865–1928)

> Turning and turning in the widening gyre
> The falcon cannot hear the falconer;
> *Things fall apart; the centre cannot hold.*
> Mere anarchy is loosed upon the world,
> The blood-dimmed tide is loosed, and everywhere
> The ceremony of innocence is drowned;
> The best lack all conviction, while the worst
> Are full of passionate intensity.
> Surely some revelation is at hand;
> Surely the Second Coming is at hand.
> The Second Coming! Hardly are those words out
> When a vast image out of *Spiritus Mundi*
> Troubles my sight: somewhere in sands of the desert
> A shape with lion body and the head of a man,
> A gaze blank and pitiless as the sun,

Is moving its slow thighs, while all about it
Reel shadows of the indignant desert birds.
The darkness drops again; but now I know
That twenty centuries of stony sleep
Were vexed to nightmare by a rocking cradle,
And what rough beast, its hour come round at last,
Slouches towards Bethlehem to be born?

PART III

WHAT WENT WRONG

CHAPTER 7

Inflation is always and everywhere a monetary phenomenon

The role of money as a cause of inflation has been a contentious issue since the eighteenth century. In the twentieth century the champion of this idea was Milton Friedman, Nobel-winning professor of economics at the University of Chicago. Friedman had a way of putting words together that delighted his followers and enraged his opponents: 'there is one, and only one, social responsibility of business, to increase its profits'; 'nothing is as permanent as a temporary government programme'; 'there is no such thing as a free lunch'; 'if you put the federal government in charge of the Sahara Desert, in five years there'd be a shortage of sand'. For inflation, his aphorism was: 'Inflation is always and everywhere a monetary phenomenon… There is probably no other proposition in economics that is as well established as this one.'[1]

There are two quite different analytical frameworks to explain inflation. One that can be traced back to David Hume, Adam Smith and David Ricardo is the role of money. Money is unique in being used to pay bills, but it is frequently confused with credit, which is used to *delay* paying bills. The quantity of money can increase without a corresponding increase in the amount of credit extended, and credit can increase without a corresponding increase in the money supply. There may be temporary increases or decreases in the price level due to bad harvests, large relative price changes in the price of oil and gas, changes in taxation, import prices and price controls, but unless money supply growth continues to increase *permanently* at a higher rate, such changes will result in changes in relative prices, not in *sustained* inflation. Inflation results from 'too much money chasing too few goods'.

The alternative explanation of inflation has its origins in Keynes's observation, made following the height of the Great Depression in the 1930s, that money wages are sticky in a downward direction. If trade unions succeed in raising wages, costs will rise and so will prices and unemployment. A combination of changes in public spending and taxes (fiscal policy) can determine aggregate demand and be used to stabilize the economy. As full employment is approached, the economy will be faced with Phillips's trade-off between unemployment and inflation (see chapter 9). The closer one gets to full employment, the greater the rate of inflation. More recently, attention has been paid to inflation psychology, namely people's expectations of future prices. If people expect inflation to continue to rise at a faster pace, that will influence both demands made by trade unions and companies' pricing policies and so become self-fulfilling.

Within this approach other cost increases apart from labour come from supply-side shocks (Covid, the war in Ukraine, labour force inactivity), shortages (wheat) and hikes in oil prices (1974, 1979) and gas prices (2022). Within this framework, large-scale econometric models have been built by central banks to explain and forecast inflation, and the Bank of England has a suite of them.

It is important to take care when thinking about what the statement 'inflation is always and everywhere a monetary phenomenon' means, and what it does not mean. It does not mean that the growth in the money stock is the only factor that explains inflation. Apart from short-term factors that can temporarily increase or reduce the price level (panic buying, adverse weather conditions, sanctions and so on), changes in the price level can also result from changes in the demand to hold money, the regulatory structure of the financial system and financial innovation.

In terms of inflation in the short term, economists have attempted to measure how near to full employment the economy is by constructing a measure of its excess capacity. When factories are closed or are working at reduced capacity and when unemployed people are looking for work, the key problem for policymakers is not inflation but warding off deflation. In this situation an increase in money-supply growth would result in an increase in total spending, an increase in output and a return to full employment before there was a rise in the general price level.

Excess capacity, however, is not easy to measure, and the failure to do so is one reason central banks underestimated the inflationary potential of their response to the Covid pandemic. In most countries, the pandemic led to a reduction in output because of lockdowns, bottlenecks at ports, supply shortages (building materials, semiconductor chips) and an insufficient number of lorry drivers. As the money stock kept increasing, these supply shortages simply added to inflationary pressures. If the supply-side constraints had been limited to a ship being stranded in the Suez Canal for a day or Le Gavroche having to close at lunchtime due to a staff shortage, there would have been little cause for concern. If, however, the canal was to be closed for longer or Brexit proved to be a barrier to recruiting staff in the hospitality sector, or if there was a rise in inactivity in the 50–65 age group of the working population, the impact on prices would be greater. If the supply constraints were temporary, a temporary upward pressure on the price level would result; but if they were longer lasting, a serious impact could be expected. And this did indeed happen after Covid struck.

WHAT IS THE EVIDENCE FOR MONETARISM?

The belief that increases in the money stock constitute an important cause of inflation was the view of classical British economists in the eighteenth century, such as David Hume, Adam Smith and David Ricardo, and of neoclassical economists such as John Stuart Mill, Alfred Marshall, Francis Edgeworth and Arthur Pigou in the nineteenth and early twentieth centuries. In the earlier part of his career Keynes was convinced of the validity of the quantity theory of money and spent six years writing a scholarly two-volume book *The Theory of Money*.[2] He subsequently changed his view because he judged that monetary policy was ineffective in influencing spending if interest rates reached a floor.

This Keynesian view was challenged by the counter-revolution in monetary economics. The intellectual basis for the revolution was the work of, among others, Milton Friedman, Edward Phelps and Robert Lucas – three winners of the Nobel Memorial Prize in Economic Sciences – and a great deal of research has been conducted using empirical evidence to support the revolution. I will simply outline three sources of evidence that I consider important: the work of Friedman; Lucas's Nobel lecture; and the work in the United Kingdom of Alan Walters, followed by Artis, Lewis, Congdon and Warburton.

As a result of conducting research with colleagues and supervising doctoral students, Friedman built up substantial empirical evidence for his case. One element of this was the publication of an outstanding doctoral thesis by Philip Cagan on hyperinflation in European countries (Austria, Germany, Greece, Hungary, Poland, Russia) after World Wars I and II.[3] This research clearly demonstrated that excessive monetary growth was key to explaining hyperinflation. Hyperinflations in Brazil in 1954, Chile in 1973, Yugoslavia in 1994, Zimbabwe in 2008, and Venezuela and Argentina in 2018 subsequently confirmed the same story. These governments never planned to have hyperinflation. Hyperinflations start from small beginnings, but governments eventually find that the only way to finance their public spending is by printing money.

In a study by Eugene Lerner, one of Friedman's students, the evidence on inflation in the 1860s in the United States – when the Confederate States Congress was financing its efforts during the American Civil War – showed that inflation rising to 10% a month was largely due to the printing presses being put to work. It was only after a monetary reform by the Confederacy that money stock growth was reduced and inflation brought under control.[4] Another important source using historical data was *A Monetary History of the United States 1867–1960*, Friedman's seminal study co-authored with Anna Schwartz.[5] The most surprising insight of this study concerned deflation, rather than inflation. The reduction in the stock of money by the Federal Reserve in the early 1930s led to a downturn in the US economy, making the Great Depression more severe. GDP fell by 29%, unemployment reached 25% and prices fell by more than 30% between 1929 and 1933. The Great Depression in the United States was a consequence of a failure by policymakers, rather than the result of market failure, in labour or financial markets.

Further empirical evidence can be found in *Free to Choose*, a book by Friedman and his wife Rose.[6] This contains a series of charts relating the growth in the price level with a lag of six months to the growth in the stock of money per unit of output for the period 1964–67 in the United States, the United Kingdom, Germany and Brazil. In the early years of this period, US public expenditure was increased to finance both President Johnson's domestic 'Great Society' programme and the increasingly costly Vietnam War. The money supply increased over the period, peaking at 9%. In the United Kindom in the 1970s Friedman noted the rapid increase in public expenditure financed by money growth, which led inflation to rise to 27% by 1975. Friedman also found a similar relationship between prices and monetary growth relative to output over the same time period for Japan, Germany and Brazil.

Over the business cycle, initial changes in the money stock will lead to changes in real output. The failure of the US Federal Reserve in the 1930s was to permit a contraction of one-third in the money stock, making the Great Depression much longer and more severe. In their book *A Monetary History of the United States, 1867–1960*, Friedman and Schwartz argue that the reason for the reduction in the money stock, when it should in fact have been increased, was the failure of the Federal Reserve to provide liquidity to the banking system. This resulted in a third of all banks failing as a falling price level increased the real value of their debt. As the value of securities held by banks fell, bank examiners had no choice but to mark down the price of government debt to its market value. The result was that a large number of banks were declared bankrupt. Over the longer term, the main effect of increasing the money stock is on prices rather than output, because over the long run the demand for money is relatively stable.

Robert Lucas was awarded the Nobel Memorial Prize in Economic Sciences in 1995, and he summarized his work in the lecture he gave on accepting his prize: 'Monetary neutrality'.[7] In the first section of the lecture he quoted extensively from David Hume's essays *Of Money* and *Of Interest*, with respect to the effects of changes in the quantity of money. He noted that an enormous amount of evidence on the behaviour of money, prices and production had accumulated over the past two centuries, and he specifically cited work by McCandless and Weber.[8] That work plots average annual inflation rates against average annual money rates over a thirty-year period for 110 different countries, and it reaches the unambiguous conclusion that long-run money growth results in long-run inflation after a time lag.

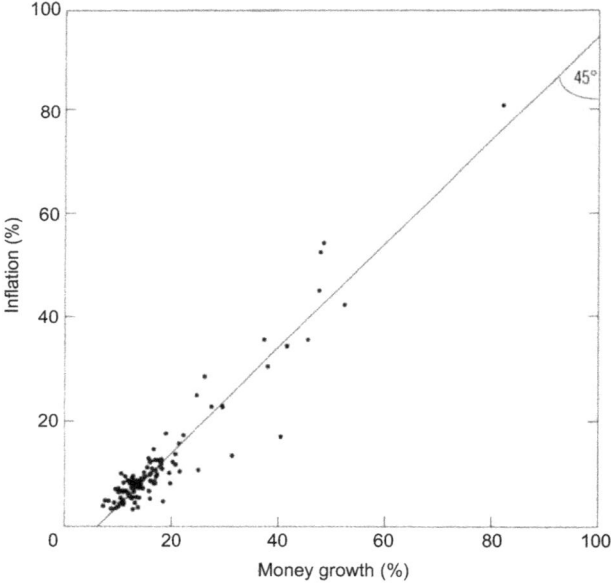

Figure 5. Money growth and inflation: a high, positive correlation. (*Source*: "Some monetary facts" by George T. McCandless Jr and Warren E. Weber. *Minneapolis Quarterly Review*, Summer 1995. Courtesy of the Federal Reserve Bank of Minneapolis.)

The third piece of evidence is from the ground-breaking work of Alan Walters and subsequent research by Walters, Artis, Lewis and Congdon, as well as by Ball, Burns and Warburton, for the

United Kingdom.[9] The most significant finding here is that, over the long term, the demand for money in the United Kingdom has a stable relationship with money income except when there is a drastic change of regime. In other words, the ratio of income that people desire to hold in money form (the velocity of money) is not some 'will o' the wisp' or a random walk but a more stable relationship. The rate of change of money income follows the rate of change of the money supply.

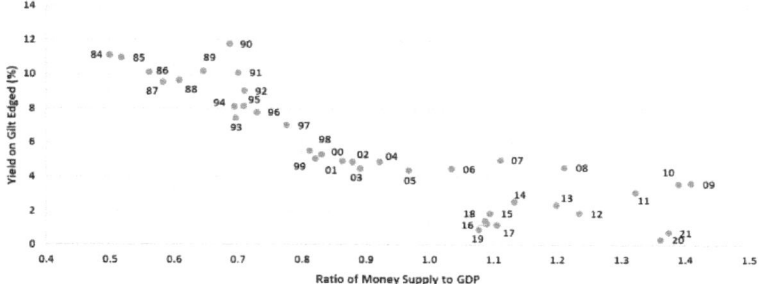

Figure 6. Interest rates and the UK demand for money 1984–2021. (*Source*: Peter Warburton, Economic Perspectives.)

Not only is the demand for money related to income, but it is also sensitive to interest rates: something that is clear from figure 5. The higher the level of interest rates, the lower the proportion of assets that will be held in the form of money. A particularly interesting finding comes from the fact that Peter Warburton used the same technique as Artis and Lewis but over the period 1984–2021 and using M4 as the measure of money. His results are shown in figure 6. In both of these charts there is a stable long-run demand for money, with the outliers (1973, 1974, 1975) being due to changes in the structure of the regulatory system (Competition and Credit Control, introduced in 1971) and shocks to the system (observations for 2008–2011) associated with the Global Financial Crisis. The rate of inflation also depends on expectations of future inflation, for which these studies use as a proxy the prior rate of inflation rather than a measure of excess capacity in the economy.

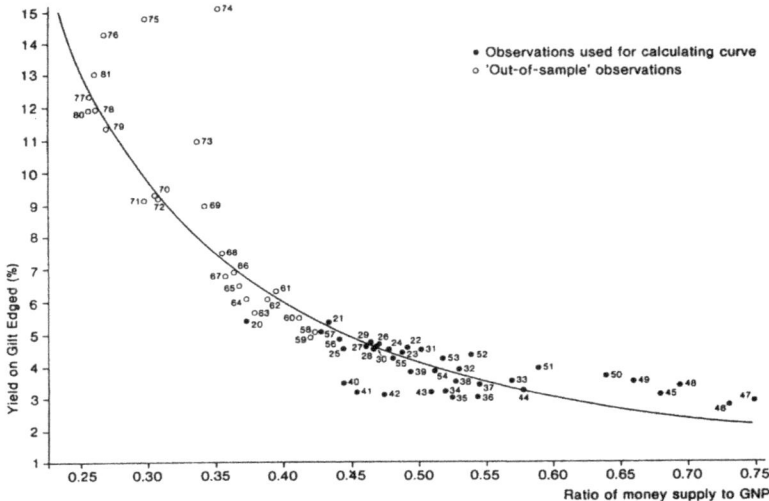

Figure 7. Interest rates and the UK demand for money 1920–81. (*Source*: M. J. Artis and M. K. Lewis. 1984. How unstable is the demand for money in the United Kingdom? *Economica (New Series)* 51(204): 474. Used with permission of John Wiley & Sons, with permission conveyed through Copyright Clearance Center, Inc.)

From the empirical work mentioned, changes in the stock of money will have different effects over different time periods. In the short term, day-to-day intervention by central banks in financial markets will provide liquidity to financial institutions in order to prevent crises from developing, but they will also siphon off surplus funds to prevent excess money creation. For serious banking crises, central banks have the responsibility to provide 'whatever it takes' (the traditional 'lender of last resort function') to ensure sufficient liquidity is available for the banking system to remain solvent.

When assessing the empirical evidence, one issue raised by Lord Kaldor and other Cambridge economists is the 'chain of causation'.[10] Kaldor accepted that there is an empirical relationship between money-supply growth and inflation but argued that causation went not from money growth to inflation but from inflation to money growth. If prices are determined by cost factors, the money supply will respond to the needs of trade because the private banking system will be able to 'manufacture' the necessary credit and money stock. In the extreme, Kaldor argued that central banks cannot control the money supply at all. The argument has validity to the extent that an increase in money income, following an increase in the money stock, will increase the demand for money. However, empirical studies invariably point to the existence of a time lag between an increase in the money stock and a rise in prices. This is the reason for monetarism's insistence on variable time lags between money growth and inflation. If government explicitly sets out to fix interest rates at below the market clearing level, monetary growth will rise and invariably lead to inflation – which is what happened in 1972–73 and again in 2021–22.

In conclusion, we can say that 'money matters'. In the long run, the demand for money relative to money income is stable, so money-supply growth will, after a time lag, lead to a growth in money income. The breakdown in the growth of money income between real GDP growth and growth in the price level will depend on excess capacity in the economy, but this is difficult to measure accurately.

The evidence of UK inflation in the 1970s and in 2020–23 is that a sudden and sustained increase in broad money growth did lead to inflation. However, the relationship between money growth and inflation over the short term is not sufficiently predictable for money supply targets to be used as a method of control by the Bank of England. This fact should not, though, be viewed as a sufficient reason for money-supply growth to be sidelined. Both in the 1970s and between 2020 and 2022, the Bank of England failed to recognize that the dramatic increase in broad money would lead to inflation.

The case for an increase in the stock of money leading to an increase in money income and rising prices is supported by empirical evidence in many countries. Changes in external influences such as the weaponization of energy prices, changes in the structure of the monetary system, or one-off changes in the public's demand for money will lead to a one-off change in the price level, but they will not cause an upsurge in the rate of inflation. A continuing increase in the money stock will lead to an increase in expenditure, and, because of capacity and labour constraints on production, it will also lead to continuing price rises: that is, inflation.

Changes in the stock of money lead to changes in total money income, and when the economy is working at full capacity, this will in turn lead to rising prices.

CHAPTER 8

The case for pragmatic monetarism

On one occasion when the well-known British journalist and writer Malcolm Muggeridge and his wife Kitty entertained us at their cottage in Robertsbridge, Malcolm asked me what exactly my job was. When I told him that I was a professor of economics specializing in money, his quick-as-a-flash reply was: 'My dear boy, I think I'd much prefer to be a possessor than a professor.'

MONEY GOOD, MONETARISM BAD

Most people have a similar visceral response: namely, they are very happy to be in possession of money and everything it can buy. Possessing money is a symbol of prosperity, security and freedom. Money makes the world go round, and it is infinitely better than barter. Those of a generous spirit would like to see others enjoying a similar satisfaction to themselves. On the other hand, people realize that we cannot all have too much of it otherwise our ability to pay for goods and services will be greater than their supply, meaning that prices will have to rise: 'too much money chasing too few goods' creates inflation. If we have too little, spending will fall, leading to recession and rising unemployment. Consequently, we need the Bank of England to control the growth of the stock of money, however difficult and technical the process might be to comprehend.

In contrast to money, 'monetarism' is widely thought of as a bad thing. I have all too often heard people say – when giving evidence over the past twenty-five years to the House of Lords Select Committee on Economic Affairs on the subject of the independence of the Bank of England – 'I believe money matters, but', growling with an almost Cromwellian determination, 'I am not a monetarist'. In 1923 Keynes wrote:

> This theory [the quantity theory of money] is fundamental. Its correspondence to fact is not open to question. Nevertheless, it is often mistaken and misrepresented. Goschen's saying of sixty years ago that 'there are many people who cannot bear the relation of the level of prices to the volume of currency affirmed without a feeling akin to irritation' still holds good.[1]

The UK establishment has always had a visceral scepticism over the significance of money: for example, the 1959 Radcliffe Report into the Working of the UK Monetary System firmly rejected the importance of money in the economy, preferring instead the broader concept of liquidity.[2]

The word monetarism only rears its ugly head at a time of bad news. During periods of price stability, such as most of the 1950s and during the Great Moderation from 1992 to 2007, when inflation averaged 2% per year in Western countries, people thought little about inflation. When inflation is unexpected, people suffer. When it is brought under control, monetarism becomes identified with higher interest rates, restrictions in lending and possibly higher taxes and cuts in public expenditure. Because of this, monetarism is not good news for the public, for business or for the reputation of the government of the day.

Three arguments are typically made against monetarism.

The first is that it is simplistic and mechanical. It is unrealistic to imagine that the economic, political and social complexities of a surge in inflation can be simplified and expressed as a single equation: such as $M = kPY$, where M is the money stock, P the price level, Y real output and k the proportion of income held as money.[3]

This view was expressed by none other than Nobel laureate Professor Friedrich von Hayek. In an interview for the Cato Institute he stated:

I don't know what monetarism is. If monetarism just means a good old-fashioned quantity theory of course it has not failed. If it means the particular version of Milton Friedman, I think it has, because he imagines that he can achieve – ascertain – a clear quantity relationship between a measurable quantity of money and the price level. I don't think that is possible… It would be a great misfortune if people ever cease to believe in the quantity theory of money. It would be even worse to believe it literally. And that's exactly what Milton Friedman does. He imagines that it is possible to prescribe to the monetary authorities a definite rate at which 'the' quantity of money must be allowed to increase. I must say I don't know what 'the' quantity of money in a measurable sense is. It has become so complex… I say this although Friedman is a great friend of mine and I admire most of his views but his quantitative approach to economics seems to me to involve a gross oversimplification of what things really are like.[4]

Hayek does not specify what he means by the difference between the quantity theory of money and monetarism. However, Professor David Laidler, in discussing the quantity theory of money and monetarism, makes the point that modern monetarists tend to regard the money supply as more dominant in causing inflation than earlier quantity theory proponents, because of their conviction that there is a stable demand for money. The quantity theory of money is more descriptive of a process, a trend, an influence, rather than a precise quantitative relationship such as that embodied in the equations developed by Cambridge economists and Irving Fisher at Yale.

A second criticism is that monetarism is an 'ism'. It immediately suggests some form of political ideology. In response to the 'ism', people immediately raise their defences. Who are these monetarists? Academic economists, libertarians, ideologues, spectators not players, with very little experience of the real world? Or maybe right-wing politicians such as Margaret Thatcher and Ronald Reagan who became enamoured with the views of scholars such as Milton Friedman and Friedrich von Hayek? Far from being dispassionate observers they have a record of opposing socialism, advocating smaller government and engineering recession and unemployment.

And the third argument against monetarism is to focus on its exaggerated claims. In my early years as an academic economist, along with others such as Karl Brunner, Allan Meltzer, Harry Johnson and Alan Walters, I believed it would be perfectly possible for central banks to control the growth of high-powered money (currency and commercial bank deposits held at the Bank of England) primarily because it was under their direct control, so that controlling money-supply growth would bring inflation under control and keep it low. We took confidence from the fact that the National Bank of Switzerland and the German Bundesbank were successful at controlling money-supply growth in this way. However, it turned out to be more difficult than expected. The Bank of England showed little enthusiasm for it. One reason the Bank was half-hearted was that it would have required a significant change in the institutional structure through which monetary policy was carried out: namely, reform and recapitalization of the discount houses and money markets.

MONETARISM AS IDEOLOGY

These charges against monetarism need to be considered carefully.

To start with, there is the charge that it treats complex issues as if they were much simpler than they really are. Even in its simplest formulation, monetarism does not consider the rate of inflation to be solely determined by money growth: it depends on the growth in real output and, in the short run, the excess capacity in the economy, supply-side shocks (lockdowns, shortages of drivers and input parts of production), sanctions (the war in Ukraine), bad harvests, and seemingly constant changes in the regulatory framework of financial institutions that influence the amount of money households and businesses wish to hold. In addition, economists who build large econometric models for the economy as a whole tend to be sceptical about the much simpler approach used by Friedman and others.

Next, monetarism is certainly not an economic and political ideology in the way that capitalism, socialism or communism are. It is not a set of ideas that links money to free markets, the rule of law, property rights or democratic institutions. It has no view on the extent of the welfare state, the size of the public sector, public ownership, privatization or the independence of the central bank. It is not right wing or left wing in terms of politics. Thatcher and Reagan were sympathetic to monetarism, but even before the term monetarism was coined, two Labour Chancellors of the Exchequer, Roy Jenkins (1967–70) and Dennis Healey (1974–79), laid considerable stress on controlling the money supply to bring inflation under control. Indeed, one of the conditions set by the International Monetary Fund (IMF) when it made loans (stand-by arrangements) to the United Kingdom in 1968 and 1976 was that the country controlled the growth of the stock of money. From a scholarly perspective, monetarism is simply about whether or not there exists an *empirical* relationship between changes in the stock of money and subsequent changes in money income, output and the price level. It is not an ideology.

The third charge – that monetarists have historically had an exaggerated view of what could be achieved in practice – I believe has some validity. Defining and choosing the right measure of money has been far more difficult than was imagined in the early 1970s. This has been partly because of changes in the structure of the financial system, such as the collapse of the Bretton Woods system (1971–73), the introduction of Competition and Credit Control (1971),[5] and the growing importance of corporate bond markets rather than the banking system as the channel for savings to be invested. This problem of choosing the right measure of money was expressed by Charles Goodhart when he was a senior official at the Bank of England in what has come to be known as Goodhart's law: 'When a measure becomes a target it ceases to be a good measure.' The idea here is that any observed statistical relationship will tend to fail once it has been used for control purposes.[6]

In this respect, the view of Paul Volcker, the former chairman of the Federal Reserve, is interesting. Commenting on Friedman's 'pure monetarism' policy advice, which was to 'find the optimal rate of growth for the money supply and stick to it through thick and thin', Volcker remarked that it 'seemed naive at best and dangerously misleading'. He added: 'Applying such a hard and fast, almost mechanistic, rule to the conduct of economic policy meant removing the

Fed's human judgement', and it also meant that the Fed would need to know precisely how to measure money.[7]

However, after Volcker left office he also stated that, in practice, monetarism had its merits:

> The simplicity of that thesis helped provide a basis for presenting the new approach to the American public… At the same time that approach enforced upon the Federal Reserve an internal discipline that had been lacking: we could not then back away from our newfound emphasis on restraining the growth in the money supply without risking a damaging loss of credibility that, once lost, would be hard to restore… We were 'lashed to the mast' in pursuit of price stability.[8]

There is value in a simple, straightforward rule, but from a central banker's perspective the demand for money is not sufficiently stable in day-to-day management of the banking system to remove the discretion of central bankers.

Controlling money in the short term has proved difficult for a number of reasons. One consequence of implementing a strict monetary rule – one that money should grow by a certain percentage over a given time period – is increased volatility in short-term interest rates. In the United Kingdom in the past, discount houses in the London money markets and stock jobbers in the London stock exchange lacked sufficient capital to take on these risks. Another problem was something Goodhart's law had identified: when the Bank started to target a particular measure of money that restricted bank lending, bankers would devise ways around it. This happened in the 1970s, forcing the Bank to change its target from measures of narrow money (M0, M1, M2) to measures of broad money (M3).

PRAGMATIC MONETARISM

Monetarism developed in the 1960s and 1970s as a challenge to the Keynesian revolution of the 1930s. Keynes had argued that in the conditions of the Great Depression of the 1930s monetary policy was ineffective, arguing that it was 'like a string: you can pull on it but you can't push on it'. You could pull on it by raising interest rates to reduce money-supply growth, but if you wished to expand monetary growth you hit the floor at zero interest rates. By contrast, fiscal policy, through increasing or cutting public expenditure or raising or cutting taxes, would change expenditure and with it the level of income and employment.

The significance of the monetarist counter-revolution is that it led to a major reassessment of the role of monetary policy and influenced the way governments attempt to stabilize economic policy. For me, the basic contention of monetarism is that 'money matters' – something that is acknowledged even by those who would not like to be labelled as monetarists. Having said that, as circumstances have changed, so there have been different approaches to the research methods used to establish the facts, different measures of money itself, and different approaches by central banks to implementing monetary policy. In addition, new tools have been added to central banks' toolkits (e.g. quantitative easing). Much as the world's major religions have within them many variations in belief and practice, the same can be said of monetarism. As new research has emerged and new events have thrown up new challenges, so I have found myself recognizing the need to take into account practical realities. Today I would describe my own view as being one of 'pragmatic monetarism', which I would set out as follows.

First, the empirical evidence over different time periods and in different countries – rich ones, poor ones; in capitalist economies and in state-controlled ones; in democracies and under authoritarian and totalitarian regimes – indicates a relationship, albeit with time lags, between the *sustained* growth of the money stock and the *sustained* growth in money income and prices. The word 'sustained' is important. In other words, increases in prices, wages and rents are the *consequence* of monetary growth and *not its cause*, and the time lags are important.

Second, there is a stable long-run demand for money in the United Kingdom such that increasing the stock of money will lead to an increase in money income. However, one of the major challenges in research is the difficulty of measuring money, as a result of regulatory changes in banking (e.g. Competition and Credit Control), shocks to the banking system (the 2008 Global Financial Crisis), sourcing of credit through markets rather than banks (new financial instruments) and structural changes in the economy (Brexit, Covid).

Third, the short-term impact of an increase in money growth will be on asset prices, such as commodities, gold and commercial metals, art and *objets d'art*, as well as equities, bonds, houses and other property. If money growth is unexpected, there will be a significant boost to output, as David Hume described. If it is expected, the boost to output will be much less.

Fourth, there is a variable time lag in the response of money income, output and prices to a sustained increase in money-supply growth. The initial impact is on the growth in output and money income, and only later will it be reflected in higher prices. Some research in the United States, Japan, India, Israel, Canada and a number of South American countries suggests that the time lag is between six and nine months; others, including Friedman, suggest that the impact on prices occurs after 12–18 months.

Fifth, the demand for money in the short term is not as stable as it is in the longer term because of all the 'noise' in the system, such as changes in relative prices (e.g. the price of gas following its weaponization by President Putin; the price of food in 2002), liquidity crises (such as in March 2020 in the UK government gilt markets, and again in October 2022 following the pension funds crisis) and following supply-side shocks such as Covid (lockdowns and supply shortages). Keeping money-supply growth within a target range in the short term is not easy, which is why the expression 'the art of central banking' has continuing validity.

Pragmatic monetarism is an affirmation of the centuries-old quantity theory of money, and we discard it at our peril – as the 1970s and the early 2000s have shown in the United Kingdom. However, Hayek's criticism that we must be careful in claiming too much for a strong empirical relationship in the short term is an important caution, and it must be taken on board. One thing that monetarism is certainly not is an ideology.

CHAPTER 9

Why did central bankers get it so wrong?

How can we account for the fact that central banks got things wrong? One possible explanation might be that the quality of central bank staff is poor. In terms of intellectual ability, the economics staff of central banks tend to be first rate and produce endless papers of interesting and mostly relevant research. Similarly, their governors and deputy governors are devoted public servants, genuinely committed to the good of society. From the evidence of central bankers I have met over many decades, this is not a credible explanation for their recent failure.

A second possible explanation, and one put forward by a former governor of the Swiss National Bank, is that the old inflation playbook no longer applies. Think of inflation as the noise from an economic engine. In the past it resulted from the engine revving too fast. Now it constantly misfires due to capacity constraints, shortages and supply-side problems (such as the initial Covid-19 lockdowns). Then the problem became more marked following the Russian invasion of Ukraine. All of these issues are significant, and they are certainly part of the bigger picture, but they in no way invalidate the empirical evidence for what actually took place. This was supplied by the Bank for International Settlements (BIS), the central banker's bank, whose considered judgement was that:

> By the time Covid struck, monetary and fiscal policy were testing the boundaries of the region of stability ... interest rates had never

been so low ... central bank balance sheets had never been so large except during wars... With the benefit of hindsight it is now clear that the fiscal and monetary support was too large, too broad-based and too long-lasting.[1]

The old inflation playbook was clearly still of value.

A third possible explanation is the unprecedented nature of the the circumstances that have faced central banks over the past few years. Most central bank staff, including those at the Bank of England, had never before experienced inflation of this kind in their careers. What is more, Andrew Bailey took up his position as governor in the middle of March 2020, just one week before the government locked down a large section of the UK economy as a response to Covid. The economy was effectively put on a wartime footing. The Bank was soon facing forecasts of not just the worst fall in output since the Great Depression of the 1930s, but the largest peacetime economic and fiscal shock in 300 years. Added to this was what has become known as the Great Resignation, with an estimated 500,000–1,000,000 workers exiting from the labour force during the Covid period. They did so for a variety of reasons: Brexit, early retirement, younger workers moving into education, employees seeking a career break. According to the Office for National Statistics, the reduction in the labour force affected all sectors of the economy, and the increase in inactivity remains partly unexplained five years later.

These unprecedented circumstances led to unprecedented measures. When, in March 2020, the government first announced policies to tackle the Covid pandemic, the Bank of England base rate was slashed to 0.1% and banks were urged to provide generous credit to companies, with loans backed by government guarantees. The furlough scheme was introduced, enabling employees to be paid while they and their employers were unable to carry on working. Public expenditure soared. Through three batches of quantitative easing – in March, June and November 2020, totalling £450 billion – the Bank increased bank deposits held by the private sector. Most economists at the time thought that these measures were the appropriate policy response to avoid mass unemployment such as was seen during the Great Depression of the 1930s. In and of themselves the measures would almost certainly have led to a temporary upward blip in the rate of inflation, perhaps of between 4% and 6%. But inflation would also have come down quickly, as expectations of future inflation would have remained unchanged at 2%. The increases in interest rates by the Bank to achieve this would have been evidence that it was determined to clamp down on inflation. Such inflation would have been 'transitory'.

Central banks have in the past faced extraordinary challenges: the 2008 financial crisis nearly resulted in the collapse of the global banking system; the eurozone crisis of 2010–13 almost led to the collapse of the euro; the September 2023 'mini-budget' of Prime Minister Liz Truss and Chancellor Kwasi Kwarteng led to a crisis for UK pension funds and a loss of confidence in the UK government.

But Covid was different. Those other crises were financial crises, whereas Covid was a supply-side shock that reputable academic institutions predicted would lead to hundreds of thousands of deaths. But even that difference is not a sufficient reason to explain the failure of the Bank of England to take the necessary action and raise interest rates until December 2021. Long before then there were clear signs that inflation was not a 'transitory' phenomenon.

INADEQUATE INTELLECTUAL FRAMEWORK

Some central bankers have been refreshingly blunt about the failure of central banks to control inflation. Here, for example, is the judgement of Graeme Wheeler, a former governor of the Reserve Bank of New Zealand:

> Central bankers globally have made serious monetary policy mistakes. They believed they could 'game' inflation expectations by having policy interest rates close to zero (or negative) while also operating massive programs of quantitative easing. This assumption proved to be widely incorrect.[2]

William White, a former deputy governor of the Bank of Canada and previously the head of the Monetary and Economics Department of the BIS, identified the problem as one of 'central bank hubris; a trust in policy frameworks, models, assumptions and their own professional competence that would eventually prove to be unwarranted'.[3]

Since I first wrote 'The spectre of inflation' in August 2020 I have argued that the reason central banks misjudged the severity of this inflation was because of their inadequate intellectual framework in analysing the problem.[4] This begins not with central banks but with the academic economics profession. Economists love building models. While these are formally written in mathematical form, they are simply an attempt to tell a story of how an economy works, and in particular to figure out possible causal relationships. If we can explain the cause(s) of inflation, we can then – partly on the basis of past experience and partly by using new information relevant to the future – develop a more convincing story and construct an appropriate model.

When statistical economic dynamic, stochastic, general equilibrium (DSGE) models were first introduced, they were like a new model of car: they were top of the range; they were ambitious; they were dynamic, in that they recognized that various elements of the story could change with time; they were stochastic in that some elements might be unexpected; and they were general, in that they modelled the system as a whole and its parts as elements of the system.[5] But the models had four weaknesses.[6]

One problem with DSGE models is that they find it difficult to capture the unique qualities of money. They find it much easier to deal with loanable funds, in which cash and bank deposits (the money supply) are just part of the liquidity of the economy: one of many short-term liquid assets. Because of this, the ability of these models to forecast inflation other than over the very short term has never been very good. Far better for predicting sharp rises in inflation has been a much less sophisticated and rather more simple approach: namely, the quantity theory of money.

When I read accounts of meetings of the Monetary Policy Committee (MPC), I still find it extraordinary that the money supply was hardly ever explicity mentioned. A word check on 'monetary policy' in the reports of the MPC from January 2020 to March 2023 could not find a single mention of money in the sense of the stock of money, money supply, money growth or monetary growth. Maybe these things were discussed but never recorded? If they were discussed they seem to have been deemed of little relevance. This raises serious questions about the diversity of thought among MPC members, and it is also suggestive of groupthink between officials at the Bank of England and HM Treasury – and possibly with colleagues at the US Federal Reserve and the European Central Bank. It is interesting that between March 2020 and September 2021 the MPC voted unanimously on its decisions regarding the level of interest rates. There was never any dissent.

A second problem with DSGE forecasting models it that they have no explanation for how inflation is determined. Over the very short term (six to nine months), forecasters can rely on prices or interest and exchange rates in futures markets as well as on the announced expectations of companies about expected price increases, cost savings and likely wage settlements. However, over a longer period, precious little evidence such as this exists.

Mervyn King, when he was governor of the Bank of England, chaired 184 meetings of the MPC. In an outstanding lecture on the deficiencies of the conduct of monetary policy, he said this:

> In the early days of the Monetary Policy Committee, we pored over various forecasts for inflation produced by the Bank staff for different interest rate decisions. No matter which path of interest rates we simulated, inflation always returned to target (2%). Why? Because in these models the only determinant of inflation in the medium term was the official target.[7]

The logic behind this was that because future inflation is determined by people's expectations of inflation, such expectations could be influenced by the announcements of central banks through 'forward guidance'. Central bankers believed that by offering forward guidance to the markets, they could influence the future rate of inflation. But what if the Bank got its forward guidance wrong? The fact is, it never does. The reason for this is that as it begins to see what the medium term looks like, it can always change interest rates or vary quantitative easing to change the inflation outcome in order to meet the official target. After a few years, the prediction of those models is that inflation will invariably return to 2%.

The Bank has a clear responsibility to explain its view of how the economy works, but given the radical uncertainty of the world in which we live, it is not in a position to give guidance regarding future interest rates and inflation other than for the very short term. Financial markets are perfectly capable of forming their own expectations from the raw data available to them and using common sense to make judgements about the future without the Bank needlessly adding additional layers of complexity. By giving this information the Bank clearly thought it was providing a service to financial markets. However, during Mark Carney's time as governor, far from simplifying the markets' understanding of what the Bank was trying to do, he famously acquired the title of 'the unreliable boyfriend', and not without reason.

The Bank has now more or less abandoned forward guidance. Huw Pill, the Bank's chief economist, has stated that there may have been a case for forward guidance in the past, when interest rates were repressed at effectively zero, and also in the transition from the post-Covid regime to one of higher interest rates, a shrinking quantitative easing asset portfolio and possible gilt sales,[8] but there is no such need now. The new approach states that 'the scale, pace and timing of any further increases in Bank Rate will reflect the Committee's assessment of the economic outlook and inflationary pressures' and also that 'the Committee will be alert to ... more persistent inflationary pressures ... and act forcefully in response'.[9] This allows the Bank greater flexibility in the face of greater uncertainties, and it gives it greater freedom to take rapid action when inflation is more persistent.

A third way in which DSGE models have 'let the Bank down' is by failing to incorporate structural changes occurring within the economy and financial system. These models cannot easily cope with structural changes in the economy due to crises, new regulations, innovation and so on. DSGE models failed to predict both the Great Financial Crisis of 2008–9 and the Covid–Ukraine inflation in 2020–22.

The fourth possible reason the Bank of England has failed to control inflation is simply because of the increasing and conflicting number of objectives it has been required to meet. The Bank's primary objective is to maintain low and stable prices, and associated with that it must ensure the stability of the UK financial system. This is, in and of itself, a huge task and a great responsibility. The Bank also has a secondary statutory responsibility: namely, supporting the objectives of government economic policy including growth and employment. More recent responsibilities that the Bank has been given relate to the soundness of individual firms, facilitating competition between financial institutions and, most recently, addressing climate change risks that affect the financial system.

Given the amount of care officials take in reaching decisions on these issues, it is not possible in practice, simply because of the constraints of time, for the Bank to pursue all these policies simultaneously. The one objective that the Bank – and only the Bank – can deliver is price stability. Other objectives must be accepted as the responsibility of other areas of the executive arm of government, and not that of the central bank.

We should not underestimate the challenges central banks faced in responding to Covid, the consequent supply-side shocks to the economy and the Russian invasion of Ukraine. Many central bank officials had no experience of dealing with high inflation. That said, major central banks failed to take appropriate action to control the recent inflation. They displayed an element of hubris, with unwarranted trust in their own models and too much confidence in offering forward guidance. Simultaneously, they were set an increasing number of objectives by government, distracting them from their primary objective of price stability.

PART IV

CATCHING A TIGER BY THE TAIL

CHAPTER 10

'Greedflation' and price ceilings

As inflation proved to be persistent, one charge the government has faced is failing to tackle 'profiteering' by companies, commonly referred to as 'greedflation'. Whether it is excessive petrol price rises by supermarkets, energy companies putting up gas and electricity prices more than is merited, or banks failing to pass on increases in interest rates to savers, the public clearly feel that companies have taken advantage of inflation to increase profit margins and to benefit shareholders and management at their expense. An Opinium survey in 2022 found that 70% of the public wanted the government to cap the price of food and essentials such as clothing, housing and transport.

Using less emotive language while giving evidence to the Treasury Committee of the House of Commons, Andrew Bailey, governor of the Bank of England, warned that 'we can't have companies seeking to rebuild profit margins which means prices continue to go up at their current rates'.[1] In a similar vein, the European Central Bank (ECB) concluded in its March 2023 report that 'the effect of profits on domestic price pressures has been exceptional from a historical perspective'. Christine Lagarde, the ECB's president, was careful in the way she described the issue:

> In some sectors, firms have been able to increase their profit margins on the back of mismatches between supply and demand and the uncertainty created by high and volatile inflation.

An IMF research paper concluded that rising corporate profit margins accounted for 45% of the inflation seen in Europe since the beginning of 2022 as companies increased prices by more than the spiking costs of imported energy. Gita Gopinath, the IMF's deputy managing director, went one step further: 'If inflation is to fall quickly firms must allow their profit margins – which have shot up during the past two years – to decline.' However, the research paper on which Gopinath's statement was based was more guarded, making clear that its conclusion was 'not the same as saying that profitability has increased' and that 'the data does not point to a widespread increase in markups'.[2]

Although 'greedflation' is an emotive expression, it certainly chimes with the public mood and has been taken seriously by politicians. Prime Minister Rishi Sunak initiated a meeting with supermarket bosses and farmers in May 2023 to discuss the price of food and how it might be brought down, and Jeremy Hunt, the Chancellor of the Exchequer, asked UK regulators (the Competition and Markets Authority, the Financial Conduct Authority, Ofgem, Ofcom, Ofwat) to examine the charge of profiteering in their respective areas.

What, then, can be said of 'greedflation'? Greed is certainly an unattractive feature of life. It is common to the whole of humanity, and the world of business and finance is no exception. It is undoubtedly the case that certain firms are more aggressive than others in their behaviour and are ready to take immediate advantage of profit opportunities, but all firms are limited by what customers will pay.

The price of milk has been a particular subject of complaint as it has increased sharply. Are the price increases a sign of profiteering? Milk is supplied by hundreds of farms, and it is sold through a variety of outlets: supermarkets, small corner shops, service stations, etc., It is an intensely competitive market. It is therefore highly questionable whether a spike in the price of milk is a symptom of 'price gouging'. Price spikes arise for many reasons: panic buying, freak supply-side shocks (such as when the *Ever Given* ship became stranded in the Suez Canal for six days), the easing of Covid restrictions for air travel. In some 'customer markets', such as food, firms are reluctant to raise prices because of public outrage from customers. If they have faced rising cost pressures over a long period and they expect further cost increases, they might use the excuse of inflation as a way of making up for past reluctance to keep increasing margins by small amounts. These are precisely the kind of market adjustments described by Christine Lagarde but they do not reflect price gouging by companies: they are simply the way markets work in adjusting to changes in supply and demand. In these situations, the imposition of price controls would have adverse consequences, namely empty shelves, queues and other forms of rationing.

The IMF's analysis does not attempt to test a theory of 'price gouging'. It is instead based on an identity: namely, that consumer prices can by definition be broken down into four parts (profit, taxes, labour costs and import prices). An identity is true by definition. The largest single contribution to price rises in 2022, namely 45%, was from business profits. If, as some suggest, this is profit-led inflation, then the theory envisages the cart pushing the horse and not the horse pulling the cart. In other words, causation has been reversed. However, most economists view the cause of this inflation as a combination of an enormous increase in public spending financed by monetary expansion and supply-side shocks reducing output, together generating 'too much money chasing too few goods'. Over the inflationary cycle profits will initially rise more rapidly than wages, while labour costs will then appear excessive as they catch up. The interesting point about the conclusion of the IMF economics research paper is that it made it clear that 'the limited available evidence does not point to a widespread increase in markups'. The horse was pulling the cart, not the other way around. Starting in spring 2020, markets behaved in precisely the way predicted by economic analysis.

The label 'greedflation' is easily dismissed as an attempt to obfuscate and politicize the process to no good effect, but it deserves to be taken seriously. After a survey of at least seven research papers on the subject – including ones from the Bank of England, the Bank of Italy, the Federal Reserve Board and some US universities – the evidence seems to suggest that industries in which powerful companies had pre-pandemic pricing power and were committed to maximizing profits were able to pass shock increases in costs onto customers that much more easily. This is a more nuanced description of the inflationary process but it does not explain causation.[3]

In the 1960s and 1970s governments of different political persuasions introduced prices and wages policies in an attempt to control inflation. Following extended negotiations with trade unions and business leaders, these policies set out 'norms' for price and wage increases. Initially introduced as voluntary agreements they tended to eventually become statutory. When first implemented they had some success, but in all cases they ultimately failed to keep inflation down. Early successes were undone by subsequent catching up.

In the recent inflation and in the light of this historical evidence, the government did not, to its great credit, introduce a comprehensive prices and incomes policy. However, it did set a price cap for domestic energy (gas and electricity) users in 2019 before inflation took off but then in 2022 introduced an energy price guarantee that capped prices at levels below what they would have been under the previous price cap.

CHAPTER 11

The cost of controlling inflation

If there is one lesson that stands out from the inflation of the years after World War II, it is the difficulty and heavy cost of bringing inflation under control. In this chapter we look at the challenges and costs associated with controlling inflation, using evidence from the United Kingdom, the United States and the EU.

In the United Kingdom in the 1970s and early 1980s – a period of both Conservative and Labour governments – inflation reached 27% and never fell below 7%. Bank Rate was raised to 17% in November 1979. Unemployment rose to more than 3 million (13% of the labour force) in 1982 and remained above 2 million until 1988. Controlling inflation proved to be a political challenge as well as an economic one. There were violent clashes between police and pickets during the year-long strike by coal miners in 1984–85, which cost 26 million person-days of work, the largest and most bitter industrial dispute since the general strike of 1926. The 1970s proved to be a decade-long conflict between the government and trade unions because of inflation.

Two features of attempts to control inflation in the United Kingdom over the post-war years were the need for higher interest rates and a consequent rise in unemployment. In 1958 interest rates were raised to 6%, even though inflation was only 4%; in the late 1960s they were raised to 8%; in 1973 to 13%; in 1976 to 15%; in 1979 to 17%; in 1989 to 14%; and in 1994 to 6%. The same pattern can be seen in the rise of unemployment. In the late 1950s unemployment rose from 1.2% to 2.3%; in the 1960s and early 1970s it rose from

1.5% to 3.8%; in the late 1970s is went up to 5.7%; and in the early 1980s it hit 12%, remaining at about 8% until the mid 1990s. Each of these periods of increased unemployment were responses to bringing inflation under control.

The cost of bringing inflation down is greater if there is a 'terms-of-trade' effect: that is, a fall in the ratio of the prices of goods we export relative to the prices of goods we import. If the terms of trade worsen – as they did in 1974, when the price of oil increased, and in 2022, when gas prices rose – controlling inflation becomes that much more difficult, as well as taking longer and involving greater economic cost.

Similar trends hold for other countries. A 2023 US study by Frederic Mishkin of Columbia University and colleagues examined the historical evidence of sixteen 'large policy-induced disinflations' in the United States, Canada, the United Kingdom and Germany. They found that reducing inflation had in each case been accompanied by a rise in unemployment:

> Significant disinflations induced by monetary policy tightening are associated with recessions. More specifically, all the 16 large policy-induced disinflations in our sample of four advanced economies since 1950 are associated with a recession. Hence in the current [February 2023] circumstances that already involve significant policy tightening an 'immaculate disinflation' would be unprecedented.[1]

The reason inflation is costly to control is that once inflation becomes embedded in an economy, it changes people's expectations of the likely path of future inflation. This influences the decisions they make in the present. Businesses and wage setters will need to form a view of the future course of inflation. Will the Ukraine conflict escalate? Will China invade Taiwan? Will the Bank of England stick to 'no ifs, no buts' to achieve 2% inflation? Even in the face of a general election? How will sanctions against Russia and China affect supply shortages? How will the Israel–Hamas war develop?

Employees will demand higher wages and salaries because, having been caught out once, they will wish to catch up and increase wages further so as not to be caught out again. Similarly, companies will want to avoid being caught out so they are prepared to raise prices just that little bit more in order to restore profit margins. Shopkeepers and supermarkets will increase food prices if they anticipate supply problems. Rents will be raised to match the increased demand for accommodation.

Governments will be under pressure to increase spending. The current UK triple lock on pensions mandates the government to increase pensions annually by the highest of either average earnings growth, consumer price inflation or 2.5%. The Chancellor will also face pressure to raise the minimum wage, as well as public sector wages: a huge bill.

Monetary policy is important in reducing total spending by increasing interest rates (Bank Rate). The need to raise interest rates in order to ensure that inflation will come down signals to the markets and the public the strength of the central bank's commitment. Bringing inflation under control involves long and variable time lags. Prices can be 'sticky', taking time to adjust. If it is to accept that demand for its products has changed, especially if demand has fallen, a business needs evidence. Some suppliers may have fixed-price contracts, in some labour markets compensation might be changed only on an annual basis, and rent reviews in the property market might be even less frequent.

A more difficult challenge for a central bank is to pursue a course of action that changes the public's expectation of the future sustainable rate of inflation. One definition of price stability is 'rational inattention', meaning a 'state in which expected changes in the general price level do not effectively alter business or household decisions'. A central bank has to convince the public that it is totally committed to achieving price stability. As the Bank of England has in recent years missed the inflation target by such a large margin and for such a lengthy period of time, the challenge of convincing the public becomes that much greater. Central banks typically start by being tough: 'no ifs, no buts' in bringing inflation under control. They start well, but when unemployment begins to rise and growth stalls – and when commentators, politicians, trade unions and academics question why interest rates remain so high – they find themselves under enormous pressure to give way.

In 2023 the IMF conducted a study of 100 inflationary shocks since the 1970s, across fifty-six countries, from which they drew three main conclusions. First, that fighting inflation takes a long time. In only 60% of the episodes studied was inflation resolved within five years, and in those cases the average resolution period was above three years. Success rates were lower if there were adverse terms-of-trade effects, such as the oil price rises of 1972–79. Second, consistency in policy was important. In particular this meant maintaining tight monetary and fiscal policies and avoiding the temptation of relaxing policy as a result of some initial encouraging reduction in the inflation numbers. Third, controlling inflation inevitably involved costs in terms of higher unemployment and lower real wage growth, but over a five-year horizon successful anti-inflationary policies did not result in higher unemployment, lower real output or lower real wages.[2]

Since Covid the Phillips curve has noticebaly steepened in the UK, US and continental Europe, with unemployement rising by a small percentage as inflation has been reduced. Far from being almost flat in pre-Covid years it now appears to resemble a vertical line.

THREE CHALLENGES FOR REDUCING INFLATION

There are three challenges to controlling inflation: creating a coherent strategy, sticking to the strategy, and introducing policies that tackle long-term structural unemployment.

A coherent strategy requires that fiscal policy must work alongside reducing money-supply growth. According to the Tinbergen principle that separate policy instruments are necessary to achieve separate policy targets, the central bank must prioritize the control of inflation by stable money growth and tackle financial stability through regulatory capital requirements in the banking system. The Treasury must set public expenditure and tax rates consistent with net public sector borrowing and stable money-supply growth over the medium term.

One good example of a coherent strategy was that developed by Sir Geoffrey Howe during his time as Chancellor of the Exchequer (1979–83). The centrepiece of his policy was a Medium Term

Financial Strategy (MTFS): a four-year programme that set out targets for public spending, tax, public borrowing and money-supply growth in each of the four years. It was sufficiently flexible that if growth slowed, the targets could be adjusted to take this into account. Professor Alan Walters, a person crucial to the design and implementation of the policy, commented that:

> It is difficult to exaggerate the importance of the commitment to the MTFS. It provided a frame of reference for all financial and economic policy. Never in the post war history of Britain had the (spending) programs and the revenue and taxation consequences been so closely associated at the highest level of government decision-making. On some occasions, as in the budget of 1981, the MTFS provided a powerful and effective discipline on policy, and gave rise to a financial rectitude which it would have been difficult if not impossible to achieve by other means. Overall, it gave a coherence to all the financial aspects of policy. And it concentrated on those elements of the financial system over which the government had considerable control – as distinct from many previous 'national plans' which dealt with concepts far beyond the reach of any government fiat.[3]

This policy was a key factor in bringing inflation down in the early 1980s. Unemployment, however, remained stubbornly high, with more than 3 million people unemployed between 1982 and 1986. This was a period during which unemployment rose in all European countries, and in some (Belgium, Ireland, the Netherlands) it rose by more than it did in the United Kingdom. The high unemployment was due to several factors: higher wage costs because of trade union bargaining power; the level of unemployment benefits, which set a floor for wages; and deindustrialization, which created a major mismatch between the skills of those made redundant and the skills required in the new jobs being created.[4]

The second challenge is sticking to the strategy and not easing the policy too soon, which is precisely what Chancellors Barber, Healey and Lawson did – with disastrous consequences. The problem with 'premature celebrations' is that they have to be reversed.

The first easing (1970–74) followed Edward Heath winning the 1970 general election and appointing Anthony Barber as Chancellor. Barber cut taxes and set a target of 10% growth for the economy over two years. This was exceptionally ambitious: growth at that rate was unprecedented in the post-war years. In 1970–71 tax receipts were greater than public expenditure. However, by 1972–3 public sector borrowing had risen to 2.6% of GDP. It was this which was the source of the rapid increase in money-supply growth that led to inflation reaching 27% in 1975. The good that had been achieved by Barber's predecessor, the Labour Chancellor Roy Jenkins, was undone and the foundations for the most serious recorded peacetime inflation in British history were laid.

The second monetary easing (between 1974 and 1976) occurred during the early years of Denis Healey's time as Chancellor (1974–79). Healey inherited public sector borrowing at 4.1% of GDP but allowed it to rise to 6.3% – an increase that was, once again, accompanied by accommodating monetary policy to fiscal policy. Sir Peter Middleton, who was a middle-ranking Treasury official at the time, later recalled that:

> It all became very serious when in 1976 we effectively went bankrupt. We didn't default but we couldn't borrow from anybody. We couldn't borrow internally. We couldn't borrow externally. The government credit was somewhere close to zero… It was a loss of confidence in UK economic management… Talking to our various allies around the world, none of them were willing to lend us money unless we went to the IMF, which was code for saying 'unless economic policy is changed'.[5]

The consequence was that, because the country was effectively bankrupt, the only source from which it could borrow was the IMF, and not surprisingly the borrowing was on the IMF's terms, which laid down strict fiscal and monetary targets for the next few years.

The third episode of not sticking to the strategy and easing too soon occurred during Nigel Lawson's time as Chancellor (1983–89). Lawson toyed with the idea of controlling money-supply growth by focusing on a narrow measure of money (the monetary base). This failed partly because of nervousness about interest rate volatility and partly because of a lack of support from Bank of England officials. Lawson then experimented with targeting M3, which was a broad measure of money, but this also proved difficult. Out of frustration at trying to conduct monetary policy through control of monetary aggregates, he opted instead to shadow the Deutschmark from early 1987. The exchange rate for sterling was pegged below the rate the market felt was appropriate, and the Bank of England therefore found itself unable to prevent a continued inflow of foreign currency day after day. This resulted in an expansion of the domestic money supply and, after a time lag, inflation. In 1983 inflation was 4.6%. By November 1990 it had risen steadily, year on year to 9.5%. It was the same old story: reflation had led to inflation. The policy of shadowing the Deutschmark was scrapped by Margaret Thatcher in March 1988.

Relaxing monetary policy too early was also an expensive lesson that Paul Volcker, the legendary chairman of the US Federal Reserve, was forced to learn. Volcker was appointed chairman in 1979 at a time when the Fed had lost credibility because consumer price inflation was in double figures, despite long-term expected inflation being only 7%. In October 1979 he announced that interest rates (the federal funds rate) would be 'free to float over a wide range'. By April 1980 the rate had risen to 17%. Pressure on the Fed to reverse these rate increases began to climb. Farmers blockaded the Fed's Washington headquarters with their tractors; homebuilders nailed a piece of timber to the chairman's chair; car dealers sent car keys in little coffins to the Fed.

By May 1980 growth had slowed and unemployment had risen to 10.8%, and even though inflation had reached 14.6% the previous month, the Fed decided to cut the federal funds rate by more than seven percentage points. Expectations of inflation remained high, so the policy reversal only created more trouble and failed to restore credibility. By the middle of 1981 the policy was changed and the federal funds rate was raised to just short of 20%.

The conclusion drawn by Mishkin and his team from this period was that:

The Volcker disinflation episode shows how costly disinflations can be, once a central bank has lost credibility for controlling inflation. This experience leads us to draw a critical lesson: should policymakers find themselves in positions where inflation is far above target, restoring credibility can require that they abandon monetary policy gradualism and raise policy rates sharply. Furthermore, the Volcker experience also shows that the cost of disinflation is likely to be high when a central bank caves too early to inevitable pressures to stop raising rates.[6]

Reflecting on his experience in his autobiography, Volcker himself comes to the same conclusion:

> A lesson from my career is that such success [when inflation stands to fall] can carry the seeds of its own destruction. I've watched country after country, faced with damaging inflation, fight to restore stability. Then with victory in sight, the authorities relax and accept a 'little inflation' in the hope of stimulating further growth, only to see the process resume all over again.[7]

The third challenge in this area is the need to supplement the main policy of getting inflation under control with other policies that offer hope to those made redundant and that address the needs of those in schools and colleges who are preparing to enter the labour market. Vocational training and apprenticeships are especially important. One of the great achievements of David Young (later Lord Young) in the 1980s – when he was a Cabinet minister in the Thatcher government – was that he recognized the skills that were needed in the labour market, and he drew on his practical experience of running a business to construct policies that would furnish people with relevant skills and made such training opportunities more widely available.[8]

Reducing inflation involves painful costs for people. Higher interest rates lead to higher mortgage repayments. A reduction in overall expenditure by households, businesses and government leads to rising unemployment. Government policies to reduce inflation must have sufficient consistency and credibility to convince people to change their expectations of the future rate of inflation. The great danger is that when inflation starts to fall governments tend to relax policies by cutting taxes or increasing spending, and reflation once again leads to inflation.

PART V

BUILDING DEFENCES AGAINST FUTURE INFLATION

CHAPTER 12

Fiscal discipline for sound money

Regardless of party politics, the United Kingdom's finances are a serious cause for concern. The ratio of public sector debt to GDP has risen from under 40% twenty years ago to just under 100% in 2024. Higher interest payments on the debt have become a significant item of expenditure. Looking to the future we need increased spending to strengthen our defences, to meet the demands of an ageing society, to improve our national infrastructure and to adjust to a warmer climate. Economic growth could be the answer, but since 2008 economic growth has averaged less than 0.8% per year. Productivity is poor, and the number of people between 16 and 65 who are actively looking for work has fallen. As a nation we are consuming more than we are producing, and we are not saving enough to match the needed increase in investment.

The Office for Budget Responsibility (OBR) is a public body, independent of the government of the day. Its task is to examine and report on the sustainability of the public finances. In July 2023 it published a report on 'Fiscal risks and sustainability', the conclusions of which were as follows:

> The 2020s are turning out to be a very risky era for the public finances. In just three years, they have been hit by [a] rapid succession of shocks [which have] delivered the deepest recession in three centuries, the sharpest rise in energy prices since the 1970s, and the steepest sustained rise in borrowing costs since the 1990s. And they have pushed government borrowing to its highest level

since the mid-1940s, the stock of government debt to its highest level since the early 1960s, and the cost of servicing that debt to its highest level since the late 1980s. From this more vulnerable position, governments face growing costs from an ageing society, a warming planet and rising geopolitical tensions – challenges that no longer loom in the distance in our 50-year projections but pose significant fiscal risks in this decade.[1]

The OBR's conclusion that the challenges to the UK public finances 'pose significant fiscal risks in this decade' rather than in fifty years' time is important, and the warning is timely.

The OBR accepts that its current forecast is based on generous assumptions: the debt to GDP ratio is to increase by 4.4% between now and 2027–28 and then fall by 0.3% in the fifth year (2028–29). This is based on the assumption that economic growth will return to just under 2% per year over the next four years, which is about double what it has been in the last twenty years. The judgement of independent forecasters is that these estimates are far too optimistic (Dr Gerard Lyons),[2] 'pie in the sky' (the Institute for Fiscal Studies),[3] and 'a work of fiction' (OBR).[4]

A further cause for concern is the risk rating assigned to UK sovereign debt by various respected rating agencies. Fitch rates the UK's debt at AA–, which is three notches below the highest possible rating (AAA), such as that achieved by Switzerland and Germany. The reasons Fitch give for this is the failure of the UK government to address the high level of debt and the weakening of its track record of policy credibility. Looking to the future, Fitch is concerned about the combination of a low UK growth rate and a level of interest rates on UK debt that is higher than we had before the pandemic.

Finally, there is heightened uncertainty over possible future pandemics, wars, supply-side shocks, network failures and financial crises.

IN SEARCH OF FISCAL DISCIPLINE

In my experience, most politicians work for the common good of society. However, they face constant pressure for the government to spend more on public services and welfare and, at the same time, to cut taxes. Because they have a responsibility to ensure that the public finances do not career out of control, they impose voluntary fiscal guidelines or rules upon themselves that place limits on total public spending and borrowing. The purpose of these rules is to strengthen the credibility of the public finances and avoid inflation.

In the nineteenth century the basic rule regarding the public finances was that the budget should be balanced: government spending should be matched by tax revenue. William E. Gladstone was prime minister on four occasions for twelve years in total between 1868 and 1894 and separately was Chancellor of the Exchequer four times between 1852 and 1882, totalling twelve years in that office. He is generally remembered for pursuing policies of 'sound finance', with the three pillars of his trinity of economic policy being balanced budgets, which matched current spending with current tax revenue; the gold standard, which ensured price stability; and free trade, which led to economic growth. For Gladstone, the national debt was original sin.[5] The origins of this approach can be found in the writings of Adam Smith, David Ricardo and John Stuart Mill. The Victorians practised what they preached. Between 1816 and 1899 the budget deficit was greater than 1% of GDP in only four years. By contrast, between 1950 and 2023 the budget was in deficit in sixty-five out of seventy-two years.

The concept of the balanced budget as a fiscal rule was challenged by Keynes in the 1930s. He argued that the rise in unemployment during the Great Depression – reaching over 20% between 1931 and 1933 – was evidence that a free market economy would not necessarily lead to full employment and that balanced budgets as a rule for fiscal discipline were inappropriate and would lead to continuing misery. The depression could only be remedied by introducing government-led deficit spending programmes: in other words, increased government spending financed not by taxation but by borrowing.

At the time of the high water mark of Keynesianism in the late 1960s and into the 1970s, fiscal indiscipline was reflected primarily in balance of payments deficits, with the result that the United Kingdom desperately needed access to foreign currency to finance deficit spending. If the government's ability to raise funds on the market became impossible, the only source of funding was the IMF – but accepting those funds meant that fiscal discipline would be imposed on the UK government, and its economic policy would largely be set by the IMF.

In 1968, following the devaluation of sterling against the dollar, the government was forced to borrow from the IMF on its terms. This meant agreeing to quantitative limits on public expenditure plans, higher taxation and control of money growth (in the form of domestic credit expansion). And then in 1976, when the United Kingdom was running out of foreign exchange reserves, the government again found it impossible to raise money on the international capital markets or borrow from other countries. It was forced to borrow from the IMF once more and, as before, it did so on the IMF's strict terms relating to the UK government's conduct of monetary and fiscal policy.[6]

When Margaret Thatcher came to power in 1979, in order to give investors confidence in government economic policy, fiscal discipline was introduced by the Chancellor through the MTFS, as set out in the previous chapter. This was not a set of fiscal rules as we use the term today. It was more a frame of reference bringing together financial and economic policy. It was a medium-term (up to five years) programme to bring down inflation on a permanent basis and to correct the structural fiscal deficit.

Fiscal rules, as the term is used today, were introduced by Gordon Brown, who became Chancellor of the Exchequer after Labour won the 1997 general election. The party had been out of power for seventeen years and, knowing it faced public scepticism regarding the credibility of its economic programme, Brown took immediate steps to establish the government's economic credentials. The Bank of England was given greater independence and fiscal rules were introduced. Borrowing was to be for investment only, and not current expenditure; the budget deficit was capped at 2.5% of GDP; a 40% ceiling was placed on the ratio of debt to GDP; there were to be triannual comprehensive spending reviews; and the assumptions underlying the Treasury's own forecasts were to be monitored by the National Audit Office.

David Cameron's coalition government (2010–15) continued with the concept of fiscal rules but strengthened them by establishing the Office for Budget Responsibility (OBR), charged with providing independent forecasts for the UK economy. Rishi Sunak introduced new fiscal rules in 2021 when he was Chancellor of the Exchequer and stuck with them when he became prime minister in late 2022 (save for one small change).[7]

In a display bordering on utter contempt for everything that had gone before, in September 2022 Liz Truss, the prime minister, and her Chancellor Kwasi Kwarteng not only ignored the advice of Sir Tom Scholar, the most senior permanent Treasury official, but sacked him. They also chose to ignore all the advice offered by other Treasury officials. Truss described Treasury orthodoxy as 'abacus economics', 'a dead hand', 'stale', 'group think' and 'risk averse'. Truss and Kwarteng did not even disclose details of the measures they planned to introduce to the Bank of England, and they paid no regard to forecasts made by the Office for Budget Responsibility either. They announced a huge package of support for energy expenditure, cancelled planned increases in national insurance and corporation tax, cut stamp duty, announced a plan to abolish the 'additional' 45% income tax rate and reduce the basic rate to 19%, abolished the health and social care levy, and removed the limit on bankers' bonuses. They then left it to the rest of the world to make a judgement on their proposals and – as the pound plummeted and interest rates on UK government bonds and mortgages rose – the rest of the world gave a resounding vote of no confidence.

SHORTCOMINGS OF UK FISCAL RULES

Fiscal rules are of value because they provide an anchor for stable public finances. However, their value depends on their transparency. They must be realistic and predictable. As they have been applied in the United Kingdom, fiscal rules have a number of shortcomings.

- They are short term, typically lasting not more than five years, the maximum length of a parliament.

- They can be changed by governments at any time. Since 2008 UK fiscal rules have been changed eight times. Typically, the changes made to the rules have been to bend them in response to changes in the financial outlook, rather than sticking to the rules and changing policy to meet them.

- OBR forecasts, like most forecasts, have at times been significantly wide of the mark.[8]

- The present system is easily gamed. The current rule requires the ratio of public sector debt to GDP to fall from the fourth to the fifth year on a rolling five-year horizon. The ratio can, however, increase by any amount between the first year and the fourth. In its projections, the OBR must accept the government's own estimates for expenditure and taxes for the third, fourth and fifth years, which might be totally unrealistic.

- Governments can propose tax increases but then fail to implement them. For the past fifteen years the government has promised in its annual budget to increase fuel duty but has yet to do so.

- Chancellors have given themselves little 'headroom' against debt falling at the end of the forecast period.

The current fiscal rules have also been criticized because they do not take into account the value of assets, such as the roads, hospitals, schools and clean water that are built or improved by public sector investment.[9] This omission, it is argued, reduces economic growth, weakens macroeconomic resilience and amplifies the doom loop.[10] However, this argument has weaknesses: the costs of potential investments almost invariably overrun forecasts (see, for example, HS2); it is difficult to measure the public benefits (e.g. estimating the potential benefits of a healthier society as a result of an increase in nurses' wages); and some assets, while being of real value, are totally illiquid in term of repaying debt (e.g. national parks).

STRENGTHENING FISCAL DISCIPLINE

The fiscal rules that have been followed in the United Kingdom since 1997 have many weaknesses and broadly speaking are not fit for purpose. However, both investors and the general public require some assurance that the government recognizes limits on its ability to spend and borrow. Truss's autumn 2022 experiment is a timely reminder of how disastrous the outcome can be when poor judgements are made.

The government has three options to try to strengthen fiscal discipline. It could modify the existing rules; it could adopt some version of an MTFS; or it could introduce a 'debt brake', such as that which exists in Switzerland and Germany.

One way forward would be to change the OBR's role in the forecasting process.[11] At present, the OBR, in making assessments for its forecasts, must use the government's own policy assumptions about its future expenditure and taxation plans. The OBR should instead be required to produce a second forecast based on its own assessment of expenditures in later years. Budget forecasts should distinguish more clearly between future investment and current spending. In addition, while long-term, fifty-year projections do have value, additional forecasts of, say, ten, fifteen or twenty years might prove even more valuable.

Another possibility would be to replace existing fiscal rules with a new version of the MTFS. This was widely recognized as a success in the 1980s in correcting public sector imbalances and reducing inflation, despite the tax increases it required having been trashed at the time by 364 academic economists. The MTFS was not a set of fixed rules: it was more a programme for reducing the public sector borrowing requirement (PSBR) through projected public expenditure plans and implied tax revenues, which would feed into a monetary and credit policy to bring inflation under control. The government set projected numbers for the PSBR for three years ahead, recognizing that the PSBR was the difference between two very large numbers. However, it was clear that if public spending overshot, taxes would need to be raised.

A third approach would be for government to place a cap on either the ratio of public sector debt to GDP or the ratio of tax to GDP. This is not a new idea. In 1946 the distinguished Australian economist Colin Clark developed an idea that Keynes himself had suggested (in the context of France): namely, that the public finances might be an important factor in determining the value of a currency.[12] Clark's proposition was that a ratio of tax to GDP of more than 25% would lead to inflation, to which Keynes responded in a letter:

Obviously as you would agree, this statistical inference is rather precarious. Nevertheless, as a practical proposition I should be strongly disposed to agree... 25% taxation is about the limit of what is easily borne.[13]

An inconclusive academic debate followed. Subsequent research has shown that it is difficult to produce a universal number for a tax burden beyond which inflation would necessarily increase. As Hugh Dalton – a lecturer in public finance at the London School of Economics in the 1920s and later Chancellor of the Exchequer in the 1945 Labour government – suggested with his rejection of the term 'taxable capacity', inflation is not conditioned simply by the volume of increased public expenditure: one must also consider the character of that expenditure.[14]

While accepting that there is no universal number to settle on, one still has a nagging feeling that there is a case for some form of cap on expenditure or borrowing. The greater the scale of the welfare state, the greater the seeming demands for its extension, whether in calls for provision of school meals for all children including during school holidays, more generous universal state-financed social care for all, or expanded pre-school provision to encourage working mothers to return to employed work. The greater the expansion of the welfare state, the less the incentive to save and, in areas in which the state is the major provider and funder of services (schools, universities and the NHS), the greater is the scope for trade unions to use their bargaining power to force wage increases.

Expanding the role for government may have a debilitating effect: taxes will rise and tasks previously undertaken by family members, friends and neighbours will be done by 'experts' under government regulations. People will be more reluctant to challenge the idea that some activities should be left to individuals themselves or to parents or family members rather than being taken care of by the state; similarly, the idea that some activities should be left to the private sector rather than the public sector will receive less support.

In 2001 the ratio of central government debt to GDP in the United Kingdom, France and the United States was roughly 50%. In Italy it was 100%. Today, based on OECD data, the relevant figures are 97% for the United Kingdom, 117% for France, 144% for the United States and 148% for Italy.[15] If increasing debt is not to be the trigger for monetary expansion, then two requirements must be acknowledged by policy makers according to Olivier Blanchard (former chief economist at the IMF). The first is that the real growth rate of the economy must be greater than or equal to the real interest rate on debt, and the second is that the ratio of the primary fiscal deficit (that is, government expenditure before interest payments but minus taxation) must not grow 'explosively'.[16] This means governments need to stick to some form of convincing fiscal discipline that acts as a brake on public spending. The source of this discipline would most likely if not almost certainly be the combined judgments of civil servants and politicians. Blanchard is particularly sceptical of fiscal rules because he believes no simple rule is simple enough and no complex rule is complex enough to deal with the problem.

THE SWISS DEBT BRAKE

Switzerland has made a serious, practical and to-date-successful attempt to prevent its public finances from veering out of control. In 2003, following a vote as an amendment to its constitution, it introduced a 'debt brake' on public expenditure, which has meant that government debt has stabilized at just under 40% of GDP. The rule is simple and transparent and prevents expenditure exceeding revenues over an economic cycle.[17] It is clear that the 'debt brake' has been an effective way of stabilizing the ratio of debt to GDP in Switzerland.

Switzerland introduced this measure because of a ballooning budget deficit: between 1990 and 1998 the debt-to-GDP ratio in Switzerland increased from 31% to 54%. The Swiss government held a referendum in 2001 in which the public voted on whether to amend the Swiss constitution: 85% of those voting favoured adopting a debt brake at federal level, and the change was implemented in 2003. The brake restricts public spending to cyclically adjusted revenues. The law mandates that surpluses must be used for debt reduction, which prevents post-budget underutilizations from being freely used in subsequent years. The objective is that receipts and expenditures should be in balance over the cycle, and therefore over the long term. The Swiss debt brake is not a simple balanced budget rule. The brake ensures that the budget is balanced each year, and it takes into account that tax revenue might be less than expected during a recession or after a slowing of the economy and greater than expected during boom years. The cyclical factor is measured by the ratio of trend real GDP to expected real GDP. The result is that government expenditure is limited by the total tax receipts it collects, after adjusting for whether the economy is above or below its predicted growth rate. A very important aspect of this is that surpluses can be accumulated during boom years so that deficits can be run during years of below-target economic growth.

The debt brake also allows for exceptions. The government is allowed to increase expenditure due to unforeseen events, e.g. Covid and the war in Ukraine, but this can only be done after a qualified majority vote in parliament. In the case of Covid, the government was given a period of six years to offset the extra spending it incurred during the pandemic. In addition, apart from under exceptional circumstances, expenditures on unemployment benefits are excluded from the cap on spending as they are themselves countercyclical.

One advantage of the balanced budget rule is that it provides a transparent framework for managing the public finances. It is important to stress that it is not a rigid rule, as it allows for exceptional circumstances and has inbuilt flexibility. The reduction in debt has meant a reduction in the interest paid on that debt, creating scope for new public investment. Surveys of public opinion show that the approval rating for the debt brake remains high. While Switzerland's credit rating is AAA/Aaa across the board, the United Kingdom's is AA according to Standard & Poor's, Aa3 according to Moody's and AA– according to Fitch (July 2024).

The success of the Swiss debt brake inspired Germany to follow suit.[18] The federal government and the *Länder* (the regional governments) are subject to Article 115 of the Basic Law (effectively the constitution), which states that the amounts they borrow must not exceed total expenditure except for investment that creates new assets. However, as in Switzerland, the federal government is able to make adjustments for the business cycle, with recessions producing reduced tax revenue and booms giving rise to above-average revenue. And again, provision is made for natural disasters and exceptional emergencies. The *Länder* are not allowed to increase their debt to circumvent federal policy. The German Federal Constitutional Court has insisted on adherence to the law, and it previously challenged the authority of the European Court of Justice in order to override it in this area. In November 2023 Germany's court ruled unlawful the decision by the government to use funds allocated for Covid in other areas.

The German experience has shown that debt ratios have been reduced during normal times, leaving room for expenditure to be raised to counteract severe crises. The success of the rules has depended, crucially, on their acceptance by the public. The rules' design could be improved by making cyclical adjustments less uncertain and by improving the transparency of fiscal compliance. The conclusion of Professors Feld and Reuter, both members of the German Council of Economic Experts, is that 'abolition of fiscal rules would hamper the ability of fiscal policy to cope with the long term challenges and prepare for unexpected short term challenges'.[19]

The ratios of national debt to GDP in 2024 reported by the IMF were 104% for the United Kingdom, 112% for France, 255% for Japan, 123% for the United States and 139% for Italy, whereas in Switzerland and Germany the figures were 37% and 64%, respectively.

CONCLUSION

In conclusion, contemporary economic debate is dogged by short-termism. General elections must be held every few years. Politicians are motivated to win and be re-elected. The public expects jam today *and* jam tomorrow. To help governments control inflation, decision makers have sought support from fiscal rules. Fiscal rules are an anchor provided they are transparent, realistic and predictable, but governments frequently change the rules, or game them, and forecasts are often wrong. At a minimum, the OBR should be given freedom to produce its own independent forecasts rather than have to rely on information on future spending and tax provided by Treasury ministers. There is a great need for increased transparency in the government's management of the public finances.

The Swiss debt brake, which has also been adopted by Germany, is one way forward, and it has successfully reduced the ratio of debt to GDP. It is transparent and straightforward. It is cyclically adjusted and suspended during exceptional circumstances. It is a strict and automatic rule and has strong public support.

If some brake on the growth of debt is not introduced in the United Kingdom, the most likely alternative is financial repression: that is, a policy with the explicit purpose of reducing the cost of government debt. For example, governments might introduce credit controls, interest rate ceilings and bank loan guarantees in place of transparent taxes and subsidies, in order to redirect resources to certain sectors of the economy. The public will be forced to buy government bonds indirectly through the imposition of minimum holdings of UK government stock by banks, insurance companies, pension funds and other financial institutions. This will lead to cheaper borrowing for the government, but the result will be a distortion of the capital markets and an inefficient allocation of capital across the economy. If financial repression is insufficient, the failure to control public spending will inevitably lead to higher inflation.

Inflation is a long-term problem and we need fiscal rules to deliver long-term price stability. In the nineteenth century these rules were not legislated by government but were part of a prevailing culture. There is a disinclination to surrender to rules that are perceived as arbitrary conventions without any foundation. However, fiscal rules can only succeed if they are backed by public opinion, which, to be lasting, must be based on long-term self-interest.

CHAPTER 13

What lessons should the Bank of England learn from the current inflation?

According to Stefan Ingves, the former governor of the Swedish Riksbank, the most important quality of a central bank is *reliability*. The public should have confidence that the central bank can deliver a stable price level, along with financial stability and, subject to that, full employment. Over the last few years the Bank of England has failed to deliver price stability, leading to a loss of confidence by politicians, business and the public in the institution's competence and reliability. In response to these failures, Andrew Bailey, the Bank's current governor, has admitted that 'there are very big lessons [to be learned] from this period ... about how we operate monetary policy in the face of very big shocks'.[1]

What might those lessons be?

FOCUS ON THE PRIMARY OBJECTIVE

I believe that the first lesson is that the Bank should focus on what it and only it can do: namely, deliver price stability and financial stability. If price stability is achieved, ensuring financial stability will be that much easier. As Kevin Warsh put it in a *Wall Street Journal* article in 2021: 'If price stability is squandered, financial stability is put at risk. If financial stability is lost, the economy is imperilled, and the social contract is threatened.'[2]

The primary objective of the Bank is to maintain stable prices even in the face of severe shocks. Stable prices are widely recognized as being the basis for achieving full employment, a growing economy and an effective functioning labour market, for anchoring price expectations, and for keeping down the real cost of servicing the national debt. Achieving price stability requires an institution that is focused on and dedicated to achieving this end.

Within a democracy the objectives of central bank policy should be set by elected members of parliament rather than by unelected officials, so it is appropriate that the Chancellor of the Exchequer and parliament set the 2% price inflation target. Having an explicit target for price stability in terms of the consumer price index introduces transparency and clarity in an otherwise difficult, technical area, and it makes the Bank's remit much easier for the public to understand.[3] Other measures of inflation and other objectives that could be used as the bank's target have been suggested, but none are as straightforward and easily understood as 2% inflation.[4] By contrast, the implementation of monetary policy is something technical and complex, and it benefits from the experience of professionals who have both competence and the knowledge gained from having lived through good times and bad. Implementation is best left to central bankers.

Achieving financial stability is a more complex issue, but it is made that much easier if price stability is achieved. It was sharp rises in interest rates to combat inflation that led to the late 2022 banking crisis involving Silicon Valley Bank and other US banks, to the demise of Credit Suisse, and to the UK leveraged-liability-driven investment pension fund crisis.

In pursuing price stability, the Bank must be seen to act independently of the policies of the government of the day. Governments will take political decisions that reflect the policies set out in their party's manifesto. They will, in addition, be forced to respond to short-term pressures and unexpected 'events' that might be political in nature. In the years before the Bank was granted operational independence, and especially prior to 1992, there is evidence that on some occasions the Bank set (lowered) interest rates for electoral reasons rather than out of economic prudence. Pursuing price stability may at times require the Bank to take painful and unwelcome decisions, so their actions must be kept separate from the political concerns of the government of the day.

Apart from pursuing price stability and financial stability, the Bank has also been given a secondary objective: to support the economic policy of the government of the day. And, as if that was not enough, the Bank also has responsibility for

- managing the failure of a bank, building society or central counterparty;

- the regulation of the stability and resilience of the financial system as a whole;

- the safety and soundness of banks and insurance companies (through the Prudential Regulation Authority);

- securing competition and growth within the financial system;

- supporting first-time house buyers;

- regulating financial market infrastructures;

- promoting innovation in the financial services industry;

- championing the United Kingdom's attractiveness as a global financial centre; and

- assisting the government in meeting its net zero carbon emissions target.

In recent evidence to the Economic Affairs Committee of the House of Lords, the governor remarked that the Prudential Regulation Committee must consider twenty-five or more 'have regards', to which the chair of the committee replied that the overall number was actually 'thirty-one or so'.[5]

By far the most contentious of these additional remits is the one relating to climate change. When Mark Carney was governor, the Bank stated with great confidence:

> Our climate change objective is to play a leading role, through our policies and operations, in ensuring the microeconomy, the financial system and the Bank of England itself are resilient to the risks from climate change and support the transition to a net-zero economy.

The Bank of England has become heavily involved in supporting the government's climate change policy, even though the Bank's Prudential Regulation Authority and its Financial Conduct Authority made it clear that the views of the Climate Financial Risk Forum (which reports to the Prudential Regulation Authority) did not necessarily represent their views and did not constitute regulatory guidance.

Climate change is a complex and contentious issue, and different central bank governors have different views. None doubt the seriousness of climate change, and a case can certainly be made that events occurring through climate change could lead to disorderly markets and unexpected changes in asset prices. Hurricane Katrina in the United States in 2005 led to more than £160 billion of damages and loan losses for financial institutions, for example. However, in financial institutions, decision making in relation to forest fires, droughts, hurricanes and so on is part and parcel of everyday policy making. By involving the Bank in setting targets above those that the investing institutions would set themselves, the government is requiring the Bank to support the government's political programme, which in turn threatens its independence.

Andrew Bailey is clear that the Bank 'is not there to make climate change policy'. 'That is other people's job, not ours,' he has said, but he added that 'climate change is a risk to financial stability in the prudential world [and] we must view it through that lens.'[6]

If central banks are required to focus on climate change, this raises questions of their responsibilities in other areas. The New Zealand Reserve Bank has already been asked to focus on house prices. What of other areas such as infrastructure, exports and technology?

The US Federal Reserve has been asked to pay attention to social inclusion. What about inequality or gender issues? If climate change is regarded as a legitimate policy concern for the Bank, there is no limit to the number of issues that could claim its attention. Central banks can only have a limited impact on climate change policy, and for this reason – and because of its political nature – climate change is best dealt with by democratically elected institutions.

MONEY MATTERS FOR PRICE STABILITY

The second lesson is that money matters for achieving stable prices.

No one should underestimate the challenges the Bank of England has faced in the last few years in the conduct of monetary policy: three major supply-side shocks (Covid, the war in Ukraine and a reduction in the UK labour force), which have created bottlenecks, shortages and reduced total output. All of these shocks were unexpected. Most economists supported the policy response of the government to the Covid pandemic: namely, to increase public spending by between £300 billion and £400 billion (equivalent to £5,500 per person) and to reduce interest rates to zero and encourage banks to increase lending to businesses.

The mystery, however – at least from an outsider's perspective – is why the Bank of England has in past decades seemingly gone out of its way not just to discard but to reject the idea that the stock of money has little if anything to do with the price level, as we saw in chapter 7. British economists who have written on this subject (including David Hume, Adam Smith, David Ricardo and John Stuart Mill, not to mention Keynes) have all recognized the importance of the stock of money in relation to prices. The significance of 'too much money chasing too few goods' is a way of combining both the demand-side and the supply-side factors that are in play. Before the outbreak of Covid, broad money supply grew at an annual rate of just over 2%. In response to Covid, public spending rose dramatically. Interest rates were cut by the Bank to 0.1%, commercial banks were encouraged to lend, and broad money growth rose to an annual rate above 10% for the next 14 months (until May 2021), and then remained above 5% for the following 12 months (to May 2022).

Emphasizing that money matters does not imply that other factors such as supply-side shocks or changes in the demand for money are irrelevant or that controlling money growth is an easy task for the Bank. It is not. In a speech in July 2022, Andrew Bailey quoted from Eddie George, one of his distinguished predecessors:

> The technical implementation of monetary policy is not at all an exact science. It operates with long and unpredictable time lags so that we are necessarily continuously straining to peer into the future, relying substantially upon uncertain economic forecasts and carefully considered, but ultimately subjective, judgements about the probabilities – and risks – surrounding them. So I welcome the Chancellor's detailed reformulation of our marching orders, which acknowledges the volatility of the real world.[7]

One positive improvement would be for the Chancellor to write to the governor requesting that he ensure that the agenda for meetings of the Monetary Policy Committee (MPC) always include a discussion of the money supply statistics, which would be recorded in the minutes and reflected in the report.

AVOID GROUPTHINK; PROMOTE INTELLECTUAL DIVERSITY

A third lesson is to avoid groupthink and to ensure there is intellectual diversity among the members of the MPC.

The MPC is one of the most powerful economic decision-making bodies in the United Kingdom. Its judgements with respect to interest rates have direct implications for the livelihoods of a large proportion of the population and indirect implications for the whole population. Its members are almost all professional economists, but within the economics profession there are differing views of the way in which money supply growth affects the economy. Ensuring intellectual diversity among the members of the committee is therefore very important.

From one perspective, the MPC cannot be accused of groupthink, and in any case groupthink is a rather pejorative expression. Members of the committee have different views, express those views openly and vote differently. During 2022 and 2023 there were dissenting votes. That is not groupthink. However, there are clear signs of groupthink on one issue: namely, the importance of money supply growth and its impact on inflation. In the period of eighteen months between March 2020, when Covid struck, and September 2021, members of the MPC voted unanimously on twelve occasions to keep interest rates at 0.1%, despite the rapid growth of the money supply during 2020 and 2021. In their Monetary Policy Report for August 2021 they made clear that 'above target inflation is expected to be transitory, as commodity prices stabilize, supply shortages ease and global demand rebalances'.

Some who were members of the committee when the MPC was first set up in 1997 have suggested that there was greater diversity then than there has been in recent years. In evidence to the Economic Affairs Committee of the House of Lords, Raghuram Rajan, the former governor of the Bank of India, explained the reason for the lack of diversity:

> There is a certain macro-monetary view that prevails in central banks and is associated with DSGE [dynamic stochastic general equilibrium] models, which rarely have a role for a financial sector, rarely have a role for money and have become the prevailing go-to models. There are a whole variety of them in the basket.[8]

The problem originated, he argued, not in central banks but in universities and among academic economists. Whatever the current fashion, that is the prevailing view in universities and it is what is taught on PhD programmes. Postgraduates are then employed in the research departments of central banks or in university departments, from which they can act as consultants to central banks. One particular weakness of these models for Rajan was the way in which expectations are formed: 'They are a complete black box.'[9] Along with Lord (Mervyn) King, he argues that, mysteriously, the predictions of these models always return to a low stable rate of inflation: typically 2%. This is because pronouncements made by central banks, such as when they issue forward guidance, are assumed to be completely credible and widely believed by financial institutions and investors.

Ensuring that there is intellectual diversity on the MPC should be the responsibility not just of the governor but also of the Bank's Court of Directors. At present there are four external members and five internal members on the MPC. The number of external members needs to be increased, while the number of internal members needs to be reduced to just the governor, a deputy governor and the chief economist. This change would prevent the MPC from increasing in size. Typically, outside members have been primarily academic economists or economists with little representation from the private sector. As the Bank has shared its difficulties in understanding the labour market, it could appoint an economist from this area, as well as recruiting senior executives with experience in business who have been on the receiving end of monetary policy.

It is essential that the Bank and the MPC are accountable to the general public. The Bank's accountability to parliament is through the governor (sometimes accompanied by senior officials as well as an external member of the MPC) being questioned by MPs in the House of Commons Treasury Committee and by those peers who are members of the Economic Affairs Committee of the House of Lords. Because of its significance it is important that the MPC should be properly resourced, as must be the two parliamentary committees that are required to hold it to account.

THE BANK AND THE TREASURY: CORRECTING THE IMBALANCE

The fourth lesson is to do with the appropriate relationship between the Bank and the Treasury.

This relationship is a delicate subject – it might even be considered one of the unwritten conventions of the British constitution. The most significant change in the past century – conceivably even in the Bank's 300-year history – was its nationalization in 1946: an episode that is easily forgotten. The Bank has continued to change since it was nationalized, through different acts of parliament and because of the differing views and styles of different governors, Chancellors and prime ministers.

In principle, there are at least three possible kinds of relationship between the Bank and the Treasury. Firstly, the Bank could be primarily concerned with maintaining price stability, pursuing a lender of last resort function in providing liquidity to the financial system, and ensuring financial stability when necessary. This would include liaising with the Treasury when taxpayers' money was required to bail out financial institutions. The other extreme would be for the Bank to effectively be an arm of the Treasury. The third way is what we have at present: somewhere between the two, with two independent institutions cooperating on the basis of 'goodwill', as a reflection of Peter Hennessy's 'good chaps' theory of UK government.

Should the Bank continue to be positioned within the executive arm of government? Or should it be given greater independence to pursue its objectives, building on the reform of 1997? If the Bank did continue to be positioned within the executive arm, it would mean parliament being involved in making appointments to the Bank's key committees, and in return the Bank having greater accountability to the public at large through parliament rather than through the Treasury and the Chancellor of the Exchequer.

At present, despite its operational independence, the Bank is very much the junior partner to the Treasury. Unlike the judiciary, it remains part of the executive branch of government.

- The Treasury advises the prime minister, who in turn advises the Crown on the appointment of the governor and members of the Court of Directors.

- The Treasury sets the primary and secondary objectives for the Bank.

- The Treasury adds new remits to the Bank's objectives through the Chancellor's letters to the governor.

- The Treasury appoints members of the MPC and has a Treasury official as an observer at its meetings.

- The MPC (i.e. the governor and deputy governors, who together form a majority of the committee) is accountable to the government for the remit set out in the Chancellor's letter.

- The Treasury, through the Chancellor, must receive a letter from the governor if inflation moves away from target by more than one percentage point in either direction. The letter must include an explanation of the reasons for the divergence.

The decision by various governments around the world to give central banks operational independence was designed to protect them from political pressure. In the United States, the Federal Reserve has always been independent of the US Treasury. It appoints its own officials but is subject to scrutiny by Congress. The European Central Bank is by its constitution independent of the fiscal authorities of member states. This is enshrined in an international treaty. I believe it is inevitable that the more closely the Bank works with the Treasury, the greater will be the pressure on the governor over time to take a very broad view of his/her responsibilities, which can easily drift into acquiescing in the political judgements of the government.

The case for the Treasury having the powers it currently does in its relationship with the Bank of England is not strong. The Bank needs greater freedom to focus on its primary objectives and to appoint those who serve on its committees. In return, the Bank should be required to be more accountable to parliament and less directly accountable to the Treasury.

Such changes would mean that

- the sole remit of the Bank should be to pursue price stability and foster financial stability, which would include its remit to resolve potential bank failures;

- the Bank not the Treasury should appoint members of the MPC subject to enhanced parliamentary scrutiny;

- the Prudential Regulatory Authority – which is, as its name states, a regulatory body – should be independent of the Bank;

- the Bank's Court of Directors should be responsible for ensuring intellectual diversity of thought within the Bank, and especially within the MPC and among the staff of the economic research and statistical departments; and

- former Treasury civil servants should not be appointed to executive positions at the Bank or as members of the Court of Directors, as such appointments run the risk of fostering a too-cosy relationship between the Bank and the Treasury.

The Bank of England has a vitally important role to play in ensuring price stability. To succeed in this, the Bank must be given greater freedom to concentrate on its mission to maintain price and financial stability, coupled with greater accountability to parliament. This requires strengthening the role of the MPC and the Court of Directors by ensuring cognitive diversity in its membership and by making the Bank more accountable to parliament and less accountable to the Treasury.

CHAPTER 14

Cultural headwinds in fighting inflation

Since 1945 the primary target of UK macroeconomic policy has been full employment not price stability. We have never had rapid inflation or hyperinflation in the United Kingdom but defeating inflation has on five occasions risen to be the country's number one priority.[1] A child born today is likely to live into the next century. During their lives, they will have to make decisions regarding their career, home ownership, savings and pensions, all of which will have long-term implications for their standard of living in later life. As a result, they will have to make judgements regarding the expected rate of inflation over their lifetimes.

As we live in a world of radical uncertainty, this raises important questions. Could the response by the government and the Bank of England to a future supply-side shock produce another bout of double-digit inflation? Even more troubling, could a future shock to the economy escalate into something much worse, such as not just 1970s-style serious inflation but far more rapid inflation even though short of hyperinflation?

In view of the OBR's assessment of the current pressures on the UK public finances, namely that they pose significant fiscal risks in this decade, the answer to the first question must almost certainly be yes. Far more worrying, though, is the second question: over a fifty-year horizon to 2070, the OBR predicts that, on its current trajectory, the ratio of government debt to GDP could well rise above

300%. In this case 'governments would need to take mitigating policy action to prevent this debt spiral from occurring'.[2]

Even though he does not explore these specific questions, Emeritus Professor Forrest Capie, a distinguished official historian of the Bank of England, has examined periods of rapid inflation, defined as inflation of 100% or more in one year.[3] Before the twentieth century, rapid inflation had only occurred during the French Revolution (1790), the American War of Independence (1785–93) and the American Civil War (1861–5). After each of the two world wars there was rapid inflation in many European countries, and in some, such as Germany in 1923 and Hungary in 1945, there was hyperinflation (defined as 50% per month and above). There has also been rapid inflation in various Latin American and African countries in the past seven decades.

After examining the evidence, Capie's conclusion regarding the cause of rapid inflation is as follows:

> This historical account presents the suggestion that severe civil disorder (or perhaps weak government) has been the critical element. Grave social unrest or actual disorder provokes large scale spending by the established authority in an attempt either to suppress or placate the rebellious element. At the same time the division in society results in a sharp fall in revenue.[4]

As we look to the future, we know from the OBR assessment that the likely demands on public spending due to an ageing population, a declining birth rate, global warming and growing security threats pose significant risks to the public finances in this decade, let alone over the next fifty years. Alongside these 'known unknowns' are the 'unknown unknowns', which are inevitable in a world of radical uncertainty. This economic background suggests that the challenge we face for the future is inflation rather than deflation, and that deflation and unemployment are more likely to be the consequence of bad economic policies by countries wrestling with inflation rather than direct threats in their own right.

Examining periods of more rapid inflation for an IMF Working Paper, Stanley Fischer, Ratna Sahay and Carlos Vegh examined evidence from 133 countries and concluded that:[5]

In sum the data show that the inflation–money growth link is exceptionally strong both in the long- and the short-run. While the relationship may not necessarily be instantaneous, nor precisely one-for-one, there can be no doubt that inflation can be ended if the monetary taps are turned off. In this sense therefore our evidence overwhelmingly confirms what every schoolchild knows: inflation is always and everywhere a monetary phenomenon. This, however, is only the beginning of wisdom – for the next question is what drives money growth.[6]

Their conclusion is that rapid inflation is typically caused by large fiscal imbalances, perpetuated by monetary accommodation to real shocks and through inflation's own self-sustaining dynamics.

In view of the current unexpected inflation in the United Kingdom, the serious inflation we experienced in the 1970s, the pressure on the public finances in this decade, and the OBR's longer-term prediction, could we in the United Kingdom face not just serious inflation but rapid inflation sometime in the foreseeable future? As civil disorder and weak government seem to be a catalyst for this outcome, to what extent do the changing culture of our society and the changing values that underpin it weaken the attempt to maintain stable prices?

CONTEMPORARY CULTURE AND ECONOMIC LIFE

We have experience in the United Kingdom of one lengthy period of price stability. Following the end of the Napoleonic Wars in the nineteenth century, the price level was essentially flat from roughly 1820 to 1914, albeit with cyclical fluctuations. From 1873 to 1896 the price level fell gently, and it then rose gently until 1914, taking it back to where it had been in 1873. The period 1830–1913 was an era of 'balanced budgets': the UK budget was in deficit in only four of those years, and even then the average deficit was just over 1% of GDP. By contrast, the budget was in deficit in eighty-four of the ninety-three years between 1938 and 2022.

Writing about the nineteenth century, the distinguished English historian G. H. Trevelyan argued that the foundation of the period's success was not just economic but was related to cultural factors:

The interval between the Great Reform Bill of 1832 and the end of the nineteenth century may, if we like, be called the Victorian Age... We must not think of the seventy years as having a fixed likeness to one another, merely because more than sixty of them were presided over by 'the Queen' (1837-1901). If any unity is to be ascribed to the Victorian era in England it must be found in two governing conditions: first, there was no great war and no fear of catastrophe from without; and secondly, the whole period was marked by interest in religious questions and was deeply influenced by seriousness of thought and self-discipline of character, an outcome of the Puritan ethos.[7]

The culture that Trevelyan describes was an overarching worldview grounded in the Christian religion with its roots in the Jewish faith. The nineteenth century had many shortcomings – women did not have the vote, university education was beyond the reach of most people, working conditions were poor – but its cultural worldview created meaning for people in their daily lives, a feeling of mutual dependence within society and a sense of collective purpose. Its values were the bedrock of the reforming Victorian political, economic and social order.

The characteristics of nineteenth-century Britain that Trevelyan observed have all been eroded or replaced: religion by secularism and pluralism, seriousness of thought by trivialization of debate, and self-discipline of character by the 'Big Me' (about which, more shortly). In the nineteenth century the Christian religion was the foundation of Western culture. In the twentieth century we lived off its capital. In the twenty-first century we are pulling up the anchor, living in a society increasingly influenced by post-modernism, even though, as Tom Holland has put it, most of us in the West, even those opposed to Christianity, are but goldfish swimming in Christian waters. Writing as a historian he states that:

> Even in Europe – a continent with churches far emptier than in the United States – the trace elements of Christianity (have) continued to infuse peoples' morals and perceptions so utterly that many failed even to detect their presence. Like dust particles so fine as

to be invisible to the naked eye they were breathed in equally by everyone: believers, atheists, and those who never paused so much as to think about religion.[8]

When I wrote about the threats to capitalism and democracy in the 1980s, the challenges came from Marx and Freud. Today they come from Nietzsche and Heidegger. Nietzsche believed in the death of God, not as the death of a person who actually died but rather as the death of our idea of God as the supreme being and creator of the universe. In his *Tale of the Madman* he relates how devastating this realization is:

> How were we able to drink up the sea? Who gave us the sponge to wipe away the entire horizon? What were we doing when we unchained this earth from its sun? Where is it moving to now? Where are we moving to? Away from all suns? Are we not continually falling? And backwards, sidewards, forwards, in all directions? Is there still an up and a down? Aren't we straying as though through an infinite nothing? ... Do we still hear nothing of the noise of the grave-diggers who are burying God? Do we still smell nothing of the divine decomposition? - Gods, too, decompose! God is dead! God remains dead! And we have killed him! How can we console ourselves, the murderers of all murderers! ... There was never a greater deed.[9]

With the death of God Nietzsche recognized that Christian morality would also die a death.

In 2018 Michiko Kakutani, a Pulitzer Prize-winning literary critic and former chief book critic of the *New York Times*, published a book with the arresting title *The Death of Truth*. In her book she argued with convincing evidence that, despite its many different strands:

> postmodernist arguments deny an objective morality existing independently from human perception, contending that knowledge is filtered through the prism of class, race, gender, and other variables. In rejecting the possibility of an objective reality and substituting

the notions of perspective and positioning for the idea of truth, postmodernism (has) enshrined the principle of subjectivity.[10]

This cultural transformation has become a crisis of meaning for people in our everyday lives. How should parents bring up their children? When is it time to give up on a marriage? How are we to face suffering and death? Along with the death of truth comes the death of all transcendent meta-narratives. So out goes the Enlightenment, rejected as a Eurocentric account of history and as advocating colonialist or capitalist ideas of reason and progress. Out goes the Marxist account of progress from primitive communism, through slave societies, feudalism, capitalism to socialism to a communist utopia. Out goes the Judeo-Christian meta-narrative – creation, fall, redemption, restoration – as recorded in the Old and New Testaments. Contemporary post-modernism is as much a worldview as the Enlightenment, Marxism or Christianity.

There is a growing recognition that the changes taking place in our culture undermine the sense of togetherness that we have: they bring fragmentation in society, disillusion with democratic institutions and the erosion of what the sociologist Peter Berger described as 'the sacred canopy' of a society.[11] They leave us more vulnerable to a breakdown of civic order and, in the economy, to more rapid inflation. This is because the falling apart, despite being ever so gradual, will place greater demands on the public finances through greater public spending on family welfare, schools, health, police, prisons, the judicial process and defence, not least to cope with the increased potential for civic disorder and a Hobbesian 'war of all against all'.

FRAGMENTATION IN SOCIETY

One consequence of post-modernism is fragmentation within society. In the US context, Jonathan Haidt has argued that the best metaphor for what happened in America in the 2010s is the biblical story of the Tower of Babel. In the book of Genesis, God confused the population's only language because of their desire to build a tower that would reach to the sky, thereby enabling them to make a name for themselves. 'Something went terribly wrong, very suddenly, in America,' according to Haidt,

> We are disorientated, unable to speak the same language or recognise the same truth. We are cut off from one another and the past... Babel is a story about the fragmentation of everything. It's about the shattering of everything that seemed solid, the scattering of people who had been a community.[12]

The phenomenon of the 'Big Me' – the obsession with self, described by David Brooks in his book *The Road to Character* – views our culture as increasingly narcissistic, self-absorbed and self-important, with a trivial example being Facebook's 'like' feature.[13]

Something has gone terribly wrong in the United Kingdom, continental Europe and the United States, as evidenced by the growing divide between the values and lifestyles of two different classes, identified brilliantly by David Goodhart as the 'anywheres' and the 'somewheres'.[14]

The 'anywheres' are the new elite. They comprise about 25–30% of the population, are highly educated, live in big cities and have a strong attraction to their own people. They are socially fluid and cosmopolitan, with progressive values favouring more immigration, multiculturalism, diversity, EU membership and globalization. Matthew Goodwin tells us that they are less concerned with promoting Britain's national interest, including 'its values, borders, tradition and culture'.[15] They dominate politics, culture and the arts. They feel virtuous in that they consider themselves morally good and enjoy superior social status and the voice it gives them in society.

By contrast, the 'somewheres' comprise roughly half the population and they are more socially conservative and moderately nationalistic. They are non-graduates, relatively powerless and less mobile, with strong attachments to the group and to particular geographical places. They have a strong feeling that they have been marginalized by society and treated with insufficient respect. They are politically disillusioned and they are more likely to vote for populist politicians. They are not especially religious but they place a high value on nation and family, they oppose immigration and they question the value of internationalism.

The Brexit vote was a rebellion by the 'somewheres' against the values, dominance and indifference of the 'anywheres'. It has left a bitter divide within British politics, with Britain now described in the media as 'a more tribalist nation' and as even more 'bitterly divided' than during the miners' strike, the poll tax protests of the 1990s or the Iraq War.

But Brexit is not the only source of fragmentation. The triple lock on pensions, the scale of student debt and the cost of buying a first home have all exacerbated the intergenerational divide. Private renters, one-person households and migrants feel hard done by in the housing market. Those correcting the language and attitudes of Roald Dahl's much-loved children's books or Ian Fleming's popular novels have created deep division and anger over seemingly irreconcilable differences over the rights of different groups, such as transgender women and feminists. The subjective nature of gender self-recognition has resulted in more than 100 gender identity choices being available for those who work in the Civil Service. The cancel culture that has prevented individuals from giving lectures or taking part in debate has proved serious enough for the previous government to introduce legislation guaranteeing freedom of speech in British universities. Most recent is the divide created by Hamas's killing of 1,400 Israeli citizens on 7 October 2023 and the subsequent invasion of Gaza by the Israeli military, which has provoked an extraordinary outburst of anti-Semitism and the renewed public commitment of Islamic terrorist organizations to exterminate the Jewish race.

DISCONTENT WITH DEMOCRACY

A further concern is the erosion of democratic institutions. Books with titles such as *How Democracy Ends*; *How Democracies Die: What History Tells Us about Our Future*; *End Times: Elites, Counter Elites and the Path of Political Disintegration*; *Deaths of Despair and the Future of Capitalism*; *Megathreats*; *The Crisis of Democratic Capitalism*; and *The New Puritans* all suggest that democracy and capitalism are more at risk than they might at first appear because trust in the institutions of democracy is being undermined.[16] In response to the wave of Gaza ceasefire protests, Prime Minister Sunak stated that 'there is a growing consensus that mob rule is replacing democratic rule'.[17]

In this context, President Trump has done untold damage in undermining Western democracy. Former Senator Patrick Moynihan's observation that 'everyone is entitled to his own opinion but not to his own facts' has been cast aside in favour of 'truthful hyperbole', 'fake news' and 'alternative facts'.[18] The attack by the mob on the Capitol on 6 January 2021 – in an attempt to negate the result of the 2020 election and for which Trump has been indicted – was a direct challenge to the democratic institutions and constitution of the United States.

For a Member of Parliament to mislead the House of Commons is a very serious charge, because telling the truth is a cornerstone of our democracy. Following its investigation into Boris Johnson's behaviour during the Covid pandemic, the Privileges Committee of the House of Commons asserted in a June 2023 report: 'If Ministers cannot be trusted to tell the truth, the House cannot do its job and the confidence of the public is undermined.'[19] Even though, as prime minister, Johnson insisted that everyone must follow strict rules that forbade such activities, the investigation found that he and his staff had neglected to do so. The end result was that Johnson resigned his seat in parliament.

The Brexit referendum was a decisive though marginal win for the leave vote, but Remainers tried to reverse Brexit. The judiciary attempted to overrule parliament, and this in turn sparked division over the independence of the judiciary. Trust broke down. Over the next seven years the United Kingdom has had five prime ministers and six Chancellors of the Exchequer – a turnover rate unknown in the previous thousand years.

David Runciman, professor of politics at the University of Cambridge, is concerned that 'Western democracy is over the hill ... we are right to be frightened: something terminal could be around the corner'.[20] He views democracy as suffering a midlife crisis and thinks it will in all probability stagger on with a long drawn-out demise. It could collapse suddenly due to a pandemic or through a network failure due to gridlock or a shutdown in global financial markets, in complex global energy supply chains, or in health or transportation systems. Barring this happening, however, we could still imagine a hollowed-out version of democracy in which it could fail but still remain intact. Democratic legislatures, an independent judiciary and a free press could still exist but fail to deliver as they should.

In the field of cliodynamics (the science of complexity), Peter Turchin claims to have constructed a model, the details of which are never fully presented, that applies the scientific method to the study of historical trends using large data sets. It predicts that the 2020s will be a decade of instability.

The real wages of 64% of the US population fell between 1976 and 2016, and Turchin claims this was due to economic austerity, globalization, weak collective bargaining, a declining minimum wage, outsourcing by corporations, deregulation and privatization. Economic inequality increased and, although he claims that democracy is the least bad way of governing, he believes that societies are vulnerable to being subverted by rising inequality. In their research, Professors Angus Deaton and Anne Case, two distinguished research academics at Princeton University, document the extent of what they term 'deaths of despair' from suicide, drug overdose and chronic illness, particularly among the US white population whose education is below college degree level. For Turchin, America has been captured by the very rich – those in the top 0.1% by income – so that the United States today represents a plutocracy rather than a democracy.

Turchin describes this process as a wealth pump that takes from the poor and gives to the rich. However, it is now resulting in an overproduction of too many well-educated university graduates who expect prestigious positions in business, media and government. This overproduction is dangerous for social stability because those involved become a troublesome revolutionary force, fighting for survival with a winner-takes-all mentality and resulting in corporate scandals, doping athletes, plagiarizing journalists and students who cheat in exams. The internet, the enormous use of smartphones and the rise of social media simply add to the instability.

Martin Wolf is the most widely acknowledged commentator today on capitalism and political economy. His guru is Karl Popper, a former phiosophy professor at the London School of Economics who advocated 'piecemeal social engineering' rather than revolutionary change. In *The Crisis of Democratic Capitalism* Wolf is reasonably optimistic regarding the future, with three chapters on reforming capitalism, renewing democracy and restoring citizenship.

However, after writing the whole text, and by the time he draws conclusions, he confesses that he has come to the view that a market economy and a stable liberal democracy are simply not possible. The appeal of the former has diminished due to financial instability, rising inequality, increased personal insecurity and slower economic growth. Capitalism has not delivered the economic security and shared prosperity expected by large sections of our society. The very foundation of democracy has been undermined by loss of confidence in the elites, the growth of populism, authoritarianism and identity politics on both the left and right, and by 'the loss of trust in the notion of truth'.

In a very moving personal preface, Wolf dedicates his book to his grandchildren and is open and honest about where he stands. He states he is pessimistic about 'this new and troubling era' because he fears for his grandchildren, who can reasonably hope to see the twenty-second century:

> I fear for what the world might then look like. I recognise the dangers of environmental catastrophe and thermo-nuclear war. But I fear just as much that they will end up in an Orwellian world of lies and aggression. This is the world emerging in China and in many other countries, even leading democracies.[21]

THE TORN SACRED CANOPY

Sociologists have long recognized that religion and the sacred – whether in myth, ritual, sacrament, doctrine or convention – have played an important role in society, while recognizing this is quite different from having a personal faith. Durkheim, Weber and Marx thought religion important but were not people who had a personal faith. In the twentieth century, Peter Berger made a major contribution to the subject with his book *The Sacred Canopy*.[22] His starting point is that by our nature human beings cannot accept being alone, otherwise our lives become meaningless. We are therefore constantly seeking to create a view of the world that makes sense of our place in it and of our existence. We are at the same time shaped by the society in which we live. In this process religion becomes an intellectually valid way of understanding our world. Behind the fragile structures of everyday life, religion provides us with 'signals of transcendence', which include giving meaning and purpose to our life and the manner in which we confront human tragedy such as chaos and death.

In consequence, religion gives legitimacy to institutions and sources that create order in the economy, society and political life. Religion is a basis for solidarity and the ultimate bulwark against disorder and chaos: the kind Hobbes described as 'the state of nature ... a war of all against all'. A sacred canopy provides a cover for the whole of a society: it permeates all aspects of culture and allows us to speak the same language to each other, not least in relation to the most difficult existential issues we face. I have heard many people say words to the effect of: 'I am not religious myself, but I do want my children to go to a church school.' They might be embarrassed if their children became devout practitioners of the religion, but they recognize the value of a sacred canopy in the life of a society as a source of values. However, the sacred canopy in Western societies has fallen into disrepair and become broken, not from the rise of science but from the overconfidence of the eighteenth-century Enlightenment, which dismissed religion as the suspension of reason and the embrace of superstition. Under the more recent influence of post-modernism, the sacred canopy has become badly torn.

Today we live in Nietzsche's world, in which 'facts is precisely what there is not, only interpretations'.[23] Nietzsche was highly critical of Christianity as a 'slave religion', arguing that the idea that the weak in society should receive the same treatment as the strong was fundamentally wrong, and that there is only one universal measure of value: namely, power and the 'will to power' – the desire of people to impose their will on others. The choice we face, he believed, was between the 'slave religion' of unselfish service and the creation of the Superman, the Übermensch, the super-human person.

Even though our society has become profoundly secular, faith still has some influence. People love attending carol services at Christmas. Both the House of Commons and the House of Lords commence each day of business with prayers. The coronation of King Charles III was a profoundly Christian service. Churches, synagogues, mosques and temples are valued institutions within communities. Many weddings and funerals still take place in church, and many people still like to have their babies baptised. Church schools are popular with parents. Faith inspires charities to undertake valuable work providing food banks, shelter, social housing and education. The sacred canopy has been seriously torn, but it has not been completely destroyed. Policies aimed at restoring the sacred canopy – such as those dealing with family, schools, neighbourhoods and personal and political freedom – are important, but they are outside the scope of this book. Even then, political programmes can take us only so far. Ultimately, there is no substitute for faith, the path to which is the Church's unique contribution.

Culture and economics are not unrelated subjects. Economic trends and events are influenced by culture, and in turn they influence culture. Religion shapes the culture in which economic life takes place. It establishes a moral order of right and wrong. It provides respect for the law and prudence in economic life, especially in relation to debt, whether that is the debt of households, corporations or government. It provides purpose in work, recognizes the value of deferred gratification and is a counter force to self-interest, competition and individualism. It sets as an objective the attainment of the common good, not simply the amalgam of private interests. A robust sacred canopy is helpful in preventing excess spending leading to inflation by recognizing the importance of boundaries.

At present our culture is being weakened by fragmentation in society, disillusion with democracy and the erosion of a sacred canopy – a process that is amplified by social media. The challenges we face are the practical steps we need to take to repair the sacred canopy of our society so that it identifies and strengthens our shared values and collective purpose and provides a foundation for economic, social and political stability.

Conclusion: lessons for the future

The first lesson is that inflation is about more than money. One of the most striking but neglected aspects of inflation is its ethical and moral dimension. This was recognized by Keynes, Röpke and Robbins, the economists mentioned earlier. The choice of words they used to describe inflation – 'confiscation', 'injustice', 'disorder', 'decadence', 'moral disease', 'evil' – is telling. Inflation is more than an economic cost or a perverse redistribution of income and wealth within a society. It is at heart deceit. It is theft by another name, and it produces a culture of distrust. Distrust leads to resentment, anger and divisiveness. As society fragments, protest and unrest are generated, which lead to civic disorder and conflict. The more rapid and unexpected the inflation, the more serious the consequences. Inflation invariably leaves a society drained, fragmented and resentful.

A second lesson is that regardless of party politics, price stability should be the priority of economic policy for every UK government. Stable prices are the foundation of economic growth, employment and prosperity, whereas a nation is made poorer by inflation. Because of inflation, prices become less efficient as signals that direct people to productive jobs and capital to productive use. Inflation has invariably been accompanied by higher interest rates, rising unemployment and stalling economic growth. As the cost of living suddenly rises but incomes and welfare benefits do not, the real cost of inflation is borne disproportionately by low-income families. Governments find it impossible to fully adjust the increase in welfare benefits, pensions and income tax bands to match increases in inflation. Asset prices rise; those without assets lose out. Wealth is redistributed in an arbitrary way. No tax specialist would ever recommend inflation as a way to redistribute wealth. Taken together these failings undermine the case for market capitalism.

A third lesson is that inflation is a monetary phenomenon. David Hume and Adam Smith set out the quantity theory of money in the eighteenth century and it still holds good. You cannot have a continuing inflation without a continuing increase in the stock of money. The increase in the stock of money may be triggered by many factors – pandemics, wars, weaponization of gas and oil, natural disasters, other supply-side shocks – but unless the money stock keeps increasing, there may be a change in relative prices but there will not be a change in the rate of inflation. Inflation will be reduced only when the monetary taps are turned off.

The primary objective of the Bank of England is to maintain price stability and financial stability. In recent years the Bank has faced increasing demands to extend its responsibilities beyond these areas. Financial stability will inevitably involve the Bank in resolving potential bank failures, but apart from this, regulation is best left to independent regulatory bodies, competition to competition authorities, and other issues, especially those such as climate change, to government. The Bank's governor, deputy governors and senior staff must be given, and should actively seek, more time to focus on their primary objective, which implies reducing the increased remits that the Bank has been given over the past decade. There must also be a diversity of cognitive views regarding money and prices among the membership of the MPC, greater independence for the Bank in its relationship with the Treasury, and greater accountability to parliament because of the present 'democratic deficit'.

A fourth lesson has to do with the public finances. The trigger for the recent inflation was the enormous increase in public spending that followed the Covid-19 pandemic accompanied by an equally enormous increase in quantitative easing, matched by money supply growth to finance it.

We live in a world of radical uncertainty. We cannot know the risks caused by future pandemics, mass migration, financial crises, great power conflict or wars. Few governments, if any, have planned to have rapid inflation or hyperinflation, and no serious inflation has taken off without the public finances being out of control. We know that at present we run the risk of a debt-interest-fuelled doom loop. We also know that the United Kingdom has an ageing population, growing health and social care needs, environmental challenges such as climate change, and a need to increase defence expenditure. The longer-term outlook from existing OBR forecasts is alarming because the predicted growth in state spending is not sustainable. And all of this is happening at a time when the institutions and values of Western civilization are under threat.

Political leadership must recognize its responsibility for the longer term as well as winning general elections in the short term. One way to tackle this would be to follow the example of the Swiss and German governments and introduce a brake on the growth of national debt relative to GDP. If we had a written constitution, this would require a constitutional amendment as in Switzerland and Germany. Since we do not have one, it is a matter of urgency to devise some alternative procedure: a cross-party convention or a referendum to achieve a similar result.

The fifth lesson concerns the relationship between inflation and the changing culture of our society. In the nineteenth century price stability was founded on balanced budgets, the gold standard and free trade. These pillars were embedded in a culture grounded in the Christian religion with its roots in the Old Testament. This culture emphasized individual freedom under law, the importance of the family in the social order, the need for a welfare society and a market economy as the engine driving prosperity.

Economics as a social science offers important insights into the behaviour of markets, but economic activity invariably takes place within specific political, social and cultural contexts. Today, social fragmentation, dwindling confidence in democracy and a lack of unifying moral values in our society are weakening our culture. We cannot return to the past, and in any case we should not try to, as the past is characterized by many challenges and regrettable episodes of its own. We should, however, recognize the benefits to our society of a sacred canopy and the need for its repair.

About the author

Lord (Brian) Griffiths of Fforestfach taught at the London School of Economics, was professor of banking and international finance at City University and dean of the City University Business School. He was a member of the Court of Directors of the Bank of England in the 1980s before leaving to serve at 10 Downing Street as head of the Number 10 Policy Unit from 1985 to 1990. As special advisor to Margaret Thatcher, he was responsible for domestic policy making. Following that he was made a member of the House of Lords as a life peer.

He later served as an international advisor and board member of Goldman Sachs International and has sat on numerous corporate boards both in the United Kingdom and the United States.

He was chairman of the Archbishop of Canterbury's Lambeth Fund and is also the chairman of the charity Christian Responsibility in Public Affairs. He has written and lectured extensively on economic issues and the relationship of the Christian faith to economics and business and has published books on monetary policy and Christian ethics. He is currently a senior research fellow at the Centre for Enterprise, Markets and Ethics (CEME) based in Oxford.

Notes

PREFACE

1 Exceptions among others were Raghuram Rajan, Nouriel Roubini, Ann Pettifor and Tim Congdon.
2 Brian Griffiths, 2020, 'The spectre of inflation', *TheArticle*, 5 August (www.thearticle.com/the-spectre-of-inflation).
3 Ibid.
4 Kenneth Scheve, 2001, 'Public attitudes about inflation: a comparative analysis', Bank of England Quarterly Bulletin, Autumn.

CHAPTER I

1 J. O'Donoghue, L. Goulding and G. Allen, 2004, 'Consumer Price Inflation since 1750', ONS Economic Trends 604, March.
2 Niall Ferguson, 2001, *Cash Nexus: Money and Politics in Modern History, 1700–2000*, p. 53, Penguin.
3 Milton Friedman, 1990, 'Bimetallism revisited', *Journal of Economic Perspectives* 4 (Fall), pp. 85–104.
4 Michael D. Bordo and Eugene N. White, 1991, 'A tale of two currencies: British and French finance during the Napoleonic Wars', *Journal of Economic History*, 51(2), pp. 303–316.
5 Theo Balderstone, 1989, 'War finance and inflation in Britain and Germany, 1914–1918', *Economic History Review*, 42(2), pp. 222–244.
6 J. M. Keynes, 1940, *How to Pay for the War: A Radical Plan for the Chancellor of the Exchequer*, Macmillan.
7 F. Capie and G. Wood, 2002, 'Price controls in war and peace: a Marshallian conclusion', *Scottish Journal of Political Economy*, 49, pp. 39–60.
8 Quantitative easing (QE) is a monetary policy tool of central banks (including the Bank of England) to inject money into the economy.

When an economy is entering a period of slow growth or recession, the central bank may cut interest rates to stimulate growth. If interest rates have already been reduced, it may use QE to create new money. The way this is done is that the Bank of England (which is the Treasury's banker) will purchase government or corporate bonds from private sector institutions such as pension funds, insurance companies or asset management companies, who will in turn will find that their deposit of new money at the commercial bank has increased. In turn, the commercial bank itself has a new deposit at the Bank of England (typically referred to as bank reserves). The Bank expects that QE will stimulate greater expenditure by households and businesses.

CHAPTER 2

1. James Tobin, 1972, 'Inflation and employment'. *American Economic Review* 62(1/2), 1–18.
2. John Kay and Mervyn King, 2020, *Radical Uncertainty*, Oxford University Press.
3. A. W. Philips, 1958, 'The relation between unemployment and the rate of change of money wage rates in the United Kingdom, 1861–1957', *Economica*, 25(100), pp. 283–299.
4. Otmar Issing, 2005, 'Why did the great inflation not happen in Germany?', *Federal Reserve Bank of St. Louis Review*, March/April, part 2, pp. 329–336.
5. Charles Goodhart and Manoj Pradhan, 2020, *The Great Demographic Reversal*, Palgrave Macmillan.

CHAPTER 3

1. Dame Clare Moriarty, Chief Executive, Citizens Advice, 2022, *Yahoo News*, 4 October.
2. Action for Children, 29 September 2022.
3. Caroline Bannock, Community Editor, 2022, *The Guardian*, 27 December.
4. Earlsfield Foodbank, 2022, *The Big Issue*, 18 December.
5. Office for National Statistics, 2023, 'Impact of increased cost of living on adults across Great Britain: February to May 2023', 14 July.
6. Legal and General, 2023, 'The Rebuilding Britain Index', March.
7. Citizens Advice, 2023, 'More than 150,000 people needed help with crisis support for the first time in 2022', January.

8   New Economics Foundation, 5 May 2022 (https://neweconomics. org/2022/05/2-2-million-more-people-will-need-to-make-sacrifices-on-essentials-like-putting-food-on-the-table-or-replacing-clothes-this-year).
9   Joseph Rowntree Foundation, 2023, 'Share of low-income households going without essentials', UK Poverty Report.
10 Independent Food Aid Network (IFAN) representing 550 independent food banks, May 2022.
11 National Institute of Economic and Social Research, 2022, 'UK economic outlook', p. 33, Winter.
12 Omar El Dessouky and Charlie McCurdy, 2023, 'Costly differences', Resolution Foundation.

CHAPTER 4

1   J. M. Keynes, 2007, *The Economic Consequences of the Peace*, Skyhorse Publishing: see the introduction by P. A. Volcker, p. 3.
2   J. M. Keynes, 1923/2008, *A Tract on Monetary Reform*, p. 25, BN Publishing.
3   J. M. Keynes, 2009, *Essays in Persuasion*, p. 50, Classic House Books.
4   Wilhelm Röpke, 1960, *A Humane Economy: The Social Framework of the Free Market*, p. 217, Oswald Wolf.
5   Ibid., p. 192.
6   Ibid., p. 217.
7   Lord Robbins, 1972, *Inflation: Economy and Society*, Institute of Economic Affairs.
8   Otmar Issing, 2002, *Should We Have Faith in Central Banks?*, p. 23, Institute of Economic Affairs.
9   Morris Silver, 1985, *Economic Structures of the Ancient Near East*, Barnes & Noble.
10 Antonio Guterres, a former prime minister of Portugal, is reported to have drawn an analogy with Jesus's words to Peter when founding the Christian church: 'Thou art Peter; and on this rock I shall build My church', modifying it to 'Thou art the euro, on this new currency shall we build our Europe'.
11 S. Herbert Frankel, 1977, *Money: Two Philosophies*, p. 56, Blackwell.
12 Ibid., p. 97.
13 Keynes, *A Tract on Monetary Reform,* p. 62.
14 Ben Broadbent, 2020, 'Government debt and inflation', Speech, 2 September.

CHAPTER 5

1. Edward C. Banfield. 1958, *The Moral Basis of a Backward Society*, The Free Press/Macmillan.
2. *Sunday Times*, 3 April 2022.
3. *Financial Times*, 24 March 2022.
4. Margaret Drabble, 1977, *The Ice Age*, p. 62, Penguin.
5. *Financial Times*, 2023, 'The Bank of England's credibility is still on the line', 22 June; *Sunday Times*, 2023, 'Confidence in Bank of England hits record low', 17 June.
6. Otmar Issing, 2002, *Should We Have Faith in Central Banks?*, p. 26, Institute of Economic Affairs.
7. Onora O'Neill, 2002, *A Question of Trust*, p. 76, Cambridge University Press.

CHAPTER 6

1. Dominic Sandbrook, 2010, *State of Emergency, Britain 1970–74*, p. 157, Penguin.
2. Ibid., p. 588.
3. Ibid., p. 594.
4. Ibid., p. 601.
5. Ibid., p. 594.
6. Ibid., p. 595.
7. Ibid., p. 610.
8. Margaret Drabble, 1977, *The Ice Age*, pp. 62–63, Penguin.
9. Kenneth O. Morgan, 2017, 'Britain in the seventies – our unfinest hour', Revue Française de Civilisation Britannique, XXII – Hors Série (https://doi.org/10.4000/rfcb.1662).
10. Ibid.
11. Alan Hoe, 1992, *David Stirling*, p. 434, Little, Brown.
12. J. M. Keynes, 1919, *The Economic Consequences of the Peace*, p. 169.

CHAPTER 7

1. Milton Friedman and Rose Friedman, 1980, *Free to Choose*, p. 254, Secker and Warburg.
2. J. M. Keynes, 1971, *A Treatise on Money*, Macmillan (*The Collected Writings of J. M. Keynes*).

3   Philip Cagan, 1956, 'The monetary dynamics of hyperinflation', in *Studies in the Quantity Theory of Money*, ed. Milton Friedman, University of Chicago Press.
4   Eugene M. Lerner, 1956, 'Inflation in the Confederacy 1861–65', in *Studies in the Quantity Theory of Money*, ed. Milton Friedman, University of Chicago Press.
5   Milton Friedman and Anna J. Schwartz, 1956, *A Monetary History of the United States, 1867–1960*, Princeton University Press.
6   Milton Friedman and Rose Friedman, *Free to Choose*.
7   Robert Lucas, 1995, Nobel Prize Lecture, 7 December.
8   George T. McCandless Jr and Warren E. Weber, 1995, 'Some monetary facts', *Federal Reserve Bank of Minneapolis Quarterly Review*, 19(3), pp. 1–11.
9   Alan Walters, 1986, *Britain's Economic Renaissance: Margaret Thatcher's Reforms 1979–84*, pp. 108–116, Oxford University Press.
10 Nicholas Kaldor, 1970, *The New Monetarism*, Lloyds Bank Review.

CHAPTER 8

1   J. M. Keynes, 1924/2008, *A Tract on Monetary Reform*, p. 74, Macmillan/BN Publishing.
2   'The Report of the Committee on the Working of the Monetary System (Radcliffe Report)', 1959. The committee was chaired by Viscount Radcliffe and members included Professor Alec Cairncross, Sir Oliver Franks and Professor Rachel Sayers.
3   In the version developed in Cambridge, England, this was that $M = kPY$, where M is the money stock, k the proportion of money income households and businesses wish to hold in the form of money, P the price level, Y real income and PY money income. In the Yale version formulated by Irving Fisher, it was $MV = PT$, in which M was the money stock, V its velocity of circulation (the reciprocal of k), P the price level and T the volume of monetary transactions.
4   Cato Institute, 1983, 'Interview with F. A. Hayek', Policy Report, Febuary.
5   In his budget speech of May 1971, the Chancellor of the Exchequer stated that he would explore with banks new techniques of monetary policy with greater scope for competition and innovation within the UK banking system.

6   Charles Goodhart, 1983, *Monetary Theory and Practice*, p. 96, Palgrave.
7   Paul A. Volcker, 2018, *Keeping at It*, p. 32, Public Affairs.
8   Ibid., p. 118.

CHAPTER 9

1   Bank for International Settlements, 2023, 'Annual economic report', p. xi.
2   Graeme Wheeler and Bryce Wilkinson, 2022, 'How central bank mistakes after 2019 led to inflation', Research Notes, July, New Zealand Initiative.
3   See William White's foreword to footnote 2 above.
4   Brian Griffiths, 2023, 'The spectre of inflation', *TheArticle*, 5 August (www.thearticle.com/the-spectre-of-inflation).
5   Oral evidence from Raghuram Rajan (formerly governor of the Reserve Bank of India and now professor of finance at the University of Chicago) given to the House of Lords Economic Affairs Committee, 6 June 2023.
6   Grayham Mizon and David Hendry, 2014, 'Why DSGEs crash during crises', *Vox*, 18 June, Centre for Economic Policy Research.
7   Mervyn King, 2021, 'Monetary policy in a world of radical uncertainty', Institute of International Monetary Research Annual Public Lecture, 23 November.
8   Huw Pill, 2022, 'Returning inflation to target', speech delivered at Qatar Centre for Global Banking and Finance Conference, Kings College, London, 6 July.
9   Ibid.

CHAPTER 10

1   Andrew Bailey, 2023, Treasury Committee, House of Commons, 10 July.
2   Niels-Jakob Hansen, Frederik Toscani and Jing Zhou, 2023, 'Euro area inflation after the pandemic and energy shock: import prices, profits and wages', IMF Research Papers, June.
3   Soumaya Keynes, 2023, 'The "greedflation" questions: what have we learnt?', *Financial Times*, 17 November.

CHAPTER 11

1. Frederic S. Mishkin, Stephen G. Cecchetti, Michael E. Feroli, Peter Hooper and Kermit L. Schoenholtz, 2023, 'Managing disinflations', p. 20, US Monetary Policy Forum Report, February.
2. Anil Ari, Carlos Mulas-Granados, Victor Mylonas, Lev Ratnovski and Wei Zhao, 2023, 'One hundred inflation shocks: seven stylized facts', IMF Working Paper WP/23/190, September.
3. Alan Walters, 1986, *Britain's Economic Renaissance*, p. 83, Oxford University Press.
4. Brian Griffiths, 2024, Was Margaret Thatcher's monetarism necessary?, *TheArticle* (www.thearticle.com/was-margaret-thatchers-monetarism-necessary).
5. Aeron Davis, 2022, *Bankruptcy, Bubbles and Bailouts: The Inside History of the Treasury Since 1976*, p. 29, Manchester University Press.
6. Ibid., footnote 1.
7. Paul A. Volcker, 2018, *Keeping at It*, p. 223, Public Affairs.
8. David Young, 1990, *The Enterprise Years*, Headline Book Publishing.

CHAPTER 12

1. Office for Budget Responsibility, 'Fiscal risks and sustainability report', July.
2. Written evidence from Gerard Lyons to the House of Lords Economic Affairs Committee in 2023: 'Serious danger that the UK will fall into a debt trap before the end of this decade', SND0034.
3. Paul Johnson, 2024, 'The Chancellor is still on track to stabilise debt as a fraction of national income in five years' time, just about, but only on the basis of a pie-in-the-sky promise to increase fuel duties', initial IFS response to the Spring Budget.
4. Richard Hughes, 2024, OBR on the government's desired paths for public spending: 'Some people have referred to that as a work of fiction. That is probably generous', evidence to House of Lords Economic Affairs Committee, 23 January, Q28.
5. Todd Campbell, 2004, 'Sound finance: Gladstone and British government finance, 1880–1895', PhD thesis, London School of Economics and Political Science.
6. Cabinet Papers, The National Archives (www.nationalarchives.gov.uk/cabinetpapers/themes/sterling-devalued-imf-loan.htm).

7   Fiscal rules 2021: (i) net public sector debt (excluding that held by the Bank of England) as a percentage of GDP is to fall by the fifth year of the forecast period; (ii) public sector net borrowing is not to exceed 3% of GDP; (iii) spending on welfare should be contained within a cap set by the Treasury.
8   In November 2020 it forecast growth in 2021 of 5.5%, but the outturn was 7.4%; in October 2021 it forecast 1.9% inflation for 2022, but the outturn was 9.1%. OBR forecasting also allows little scope for changes in government spending plans and taxes to have much impact on the growth of the economy.
9   Neetha Suresh, Rachel Ghaw, Ronnie Obeng-Osei and Tom Wickstead, 2024, 'Public investment and potential output', Office for Budget Responsibility Discussion Paper 5, August (https://obr.uk/docs/dlm_uploads/Public-investment-and-potential-output_August-2024.pdf).
10 Andy Haldane, 2023, 'The case for rethinking fiscal rules is overwhelming', *Financial Times*, Opinion, 16 May.
11 Gemma Tetlow, Olly Bartrum and Thomas Pope, 2024, 'Strengthening the UK's fiscal framework', Analysis Paper, Institute for Government, February.
12 'The proportion of his earned income which the French taxpayer will permit to be taken from him to pay the claims of the French rentier', The Nation and Athenaeum, 9 January 1926; Colin Clark, 1945, 'Public finances and changes in the value of money', *Economic Journal*, 55(220), pp. 371–389; Joseph A. Pechman and Thomas Mayer, 1952, 'Mr. Colin Clark on the limits of taxation', *Review of Economics and Statistics*, 34(3); Dan Throop Smith, 1952, 'Note on inflationary consequences of high taxation', *Review of Economics and Statistics*, 34(3).
13 Ibid.
14 Hugh Dalton, 1954, *Principles of Public Finance*, Routledge and Kegan Paul.
15 General Government Debt, OECD, 2023.
16 Robert Armstrong and Ethan Wu, 2023, 'Olivier Blanchard on debt explosions', *Financial Times*, 17 Novmber.
17 Federal Department of Finance (Switzerland), 2023, 'Swiss debt brake', August; Stephan Danninger, 2002, 'A new rule: the Swiss debt brake', IMF Working Paper WP/02/18, January.
18 Federal Ministry of Finance (Germany), 25 February 2022, 'Germany's federal debt rule (debt brake)'.

19 Lars P. Feld and Wolf Heinrich Reuter, 2021, 'The German "debt brake": success factors and challenges', Freiburger Diskussionspapiere zur Ordnungsökonomik 21/10, Albert-Ludwigs-Universität Freiburg.

CHAPTER 13

1 House of Commons Select Committee on Treasury Affairs, 23 May 2023.
2 Kevin Warsh, 2021, *Wall Street Journal*, 12 December.
3 The Bank's official target measure is the consumer price index (CPI), which stands at 10.5% (February 2023). The retail price index that excludes mortgage interest payments (RPIX) is 12.9%. If these payments are included, it is 13.4%. The Office for National Statistics (ONS) measures its own 'official' figure: the Consumer Prices Index including owner occupiers' housing costs (CPIH), which is 9.2%. So we have a range of inflation figures from 9.2% to 13.4%. The problem with the figure most favoured by the ONS is that it uses imputed rent as the basis for capturing the rent someone might have had to pay if they did not own their own home. Because it is imputed, not observed, few people care to use this measure. Andrew Sentance, 2023, 'Confused about the rate of inflation? You have every right to be', *The Times*, 23 January.
4 Ben Bernanke, former chairman of the Fed, mentions the price level itself: that is, setting the price level rather than the rate of inflation as the target, then monitoring the price level from year to year, starting from some arbitrary initial point. (See Ben Bernanke, 2022, *21st Century Monetary Policy*, p. 344, W. W. Norton.) Another approach that has been canvassed in the UK is to target nominal GDP, that is, the total value of goods and services produced within the UK. This is the sum of the growth rate of real output and the rate of inflation. Its supporters claim it has potential advantages because by targeting a number it demonstrates that the central bank is concerned about both the real growth of the economy and employment as well as rising prices. For example, if the economy suffers a real shock and real growth slows, targeting money GDP will automatically lead to an easing of monetary policy, which should raise output and growth.
5 House of Lords Select Committee on Economic Affairs, 17 November 2023, 'Making an independent Bank of England work better', paragraphs 83 and 85.

6 House of Lords Select Committee on Economic Affairs, 6 June 2023, evidence from Andrew Bailey.
7 House of Lords Select Committee on Economic Affairs, 6 June 2023.
8 House of Lords Select Committee on Economic Affairs, 6 June 2023, evidence from Raghuram Rajan (evidence session no. 9, question 140).
9 Ibid., p. 141.

CHAPTER 14

1 (1) In the late 1950s three Treasury ministers, including Chancellor of the Exchequer Peter Thorneycroft, Enoch Powell and Nigel Birch, resigned, despite the increase in Bank Rate being to only 6%. (2) In the 1960s when unemployment rose but contrary to expectations so did inflation. (3) In the 1970s when inflation reached 27%. (4) In the late 1980s and early 1990s following Nigel Lawson's shadowing of the Deutschemark. (5) Since 2021 following rapid monetary expansion triggered by ballooning public expenditure in response to the Covid shock.
2 Office for Budget Responsibility, 2024, 'Fiscal risks and sustainability', September, Executive summary, p. 3, CP 1142.
3 Forrest Capie, 1986, *Conditions in Which Very Rapid Inflation Has Appeared*, Carnegie-Rochester Conference Series on Public Policy, volume 24, pp. 115–168, Elsevier. In contrast to rapid inflation, Philip Cagan's definition of hyperinflation as price rises exceeding 50% per month and accelerating and then finishing when the rate dropped below that and was decelerating is now widely accepted.
4 Ibid.
5 Stanley Fischer, Ratna Sahay and Carol Vegh, 2002, 'Modern hyper- and high inflations', IMF Working Paper WP/02/197 (corrected 31 January 2003).
6 Ibid.
7 G. M. Trevelyan, 1942, *English Social History*, quoted in S. Herbert Frankel, 1977, *Money: Two Philosophies*, Blackwell.
8 Tom Holland, 2019, *Dominion*, p. 517, Abacus.
9 Friedrich Nietzsche, 2001 (originally published 1882/1887), 'Parable of the madman', in *The Gay Science*, para. 125, pp. 119–120, Cambridge University Press (https://www.holybooks.com/wp-content/uploads/The-Gay-Science-by-Friedrich-Nietzsche.pdf).
10 Michiko Kakutani, 2018, *The Death of Truth*, pp. 47–48, William Collins.

11 Peter L. Berger, 1967, *The Sacred Canopy*, Anchor Books/Random House.
12 Jonathan Haidt, 2022, 'Why the past 10 years of American life have been uniquely stupid', *The Atlantic*, May.
13 David Brooks, 2015, *The Road to Character*, Allen Lane/Penguin.
14 David Goodhart, 2017, *The Road to Somewhere*, Penguin.
15 Matthew Goodwin, 2023, *Values, Voice and Virtue*, Penguin.
16 David Runciman, 2019, *How Democracy Ends*, Profile Books. Steven Levitsky and Daniel Ziblatt, 2018, *How Democracies Die: What History Tells Us about Our Future*, Penguin. Peter Turchin, 2023, *End Times: Elites, Counter Elites and the Path of Political Disintegration*, Allen Lane. Anne Case and Angus Deaton, 2020. *Deaths of Despair and the Future of Capitalism*, Princeton University Press. Nouriel Roubini, 2022, *Megathreats*, John Murray. Martin Wolf, *The Crisis of Democratic Capitalism*, Allen Lane. Andrew Doyle, 2022, *The New Puritans*, Constable.
17 *The Times*, 28 February 2024.
18 Kellyanne Conway, 2017, Meet the Press Interview, 22 January.
19 House of Commons, 2023, Committee of Privileges Report into Boris Johnson, 29 June.
20 David Runciman, *How Democracy Ends*, p. 216.
21 Martin Wolf, *The Crisis of Democratic Capitalism*, p. xx.
22 Peter L. Berger, *The Sacred Canopy*.
23 Friedrich Nietzsche, 2017, *The Will to Power*, translation by R. Kevin Hill and Michael A. Scarpitti, paragraph 481, Penguin.

Index

American Civil War, 45, 62, 128

Banfield, Edward, 41, 44, 150n
Bank of England
    Bailey, Andrew (governor), 78, 87, 115, 118, 120, 122–125, 142, 152n, 156n
    climate change, 83, 118–119, 142–143
    DGSE models, 80–83, 121, 152n
    groupthink, 81, 120–122
    Monetary Policy Committee (MPC), 80–81, 120–125, 142, 152n, 153n, 155n, 156n
Berger, Peter, 132, 137, 157n
Bordo, Michael D., 5, 147n
Bretton Woods, 7–8, 19, 36, 73
Brooks, David, 133, 157n
budget (UK Treasury)
    of 1941, 6
    of May 1971, 151
    of 1981, 95
    of 2021, 39
    of September 2023, 79
    balanced budgets, 105, 112, 129–130, 143

Bundesbank, 19, 35, 72

Capie, Forrest, xiii, 7, 128, 147n, 156n
capitalism, xi, 31–33, 72, 131–132, 134, 136–137, 142, 157n
Carney, Mark, 82, 118
Case, Anne, 136, 157n
Chicago School of Economics, 17
Christian, 130–132, 138–139, 143, 145, 149n
    Judeo-Christian, 132
Christianity, 130–132, 138
Clark, Colin, 109, 154n
climate change, 83, 118–119, 142–143
Congdon, Tim, 62, 64, 147n
cost of living, ix–xi, 16, 23–29, 31, 43, 52, 141, 148n
Covid-19, ix, x, xiii, 3–4, 9, 10–11, 17–18, 21, 25, 31, 60–61, 76–79, 82–83, 88, 94, 112, 113, 119, 121, 135, 142, 156n
credit rating agencies, 112
culture, 114, 129–130, 132–133, 138, 143
    culture of distrust, xi–xii, 43–47, 54, 141

Dalton, Hugh, 110, 154n
Deaton, Angus, 136, 157n
debt brake
  Swiss debt brake, 111–114, 143, 154n
  German debt brake, 109, 112, 114, 143, 154n
democracy, xi, xii, 34–35, 37, 51, 54, 116, 131, 134–137, 139, 143, 157n
Deutschmark, 97
dollar, 3, 7–8, 12, 36–37, 106
Drabble, Margaret, 43, 52, 150n
DSGE (dynamic stochastic general equilibrium) models, 80–82, 121, 152n

Economic Affairs Committee (Lords Select Committee), xiii, 70, 117, 122, 152n, 153n, 155n, 156n
energy
  costs, 24, 26–27, 30, 103, 152n
  weaponization, 11, 67, 142
  companies, 11, 87, 136
  price cap guarantee, 25, 28, 90, 107

Fiscal rules, xii, 105–109, 111, 113–114, 154n
Fisher, Irving, 71, 151n
Fischer, Stanley, 128, 156n
food banks, 11, 23, 26–28, 30, 76, 87, 93, 139, 149n
fragmentation, 132–134, 139, 143

Frankel, Herbert S., 9, 37, 149n, 156n
Friedman, Milton, 59, 62–63, 71–73, 76, 147n, 150n, 151n
Friedman, Rose, 63, 150n, 151n

GB75, 53
gold standard, 5, 7, 12, 36, 45, 105, 145
Goodhart, Charles, xiii, 20, 45, 73–74, 148n, 152n
Goodhart, David, 133, 157n
Great Depression 1930s, 31, 36, 60, 62–63, 74, 78, 105
greedflation, 87–89, 152
groupthink, 81, 120–121

Haidt, Jonathan, 132–133, 157n
Haldane, Andy, 154n
Hayek, Friedrich, ix, 70–71, 76, 151n
Healey, Denis, 9, 73, 95–96
Holland, Tom, 130, 156n
Howe, Lord (Sir Geoffrey), 20, 94
Hume, David, 59, 61, 63, 76, 119, 142
Hunt, Jeremy, 88
hyperinflation, xi, 3, 34–35, 50, 55, 62, 127, 128, 142, 151n, 156n

inflation
  2% target rate, 37, 44, 70, 79, 81, 104, 119, 121
  deceit, 31–40

inflation tax, xi, 12, 33,
    37–40, 142
greedflation, 87–90
profiteering, 33, 43
social fabric, xi
wars, 3–12
Issing, Otmar, 35, 45, 148n, 149n,
    150n

Jenkins, Roy, 8–9, 49–50, 52, 54,
    73, 96
Johnson, Boris, 135, 157n
Johnson, Lyndon B., 7

Kakutani, Michiko, 131, 156n
Kaldor, Lord (Nicholas), 66–67,
    151n
Kay, John, 17, 148n
Kennedy, John F., 7, 20
Keynes, John Maynard, 6,
    19, 31–33, 37–38, 55,
    60–61, 70, 74, 105, 109,
    119, 141, 147n, 149n,
    150n, 151n
King, Lord (Mervyn), xiii, 17, 81,
    121, 148n, 152n
Kwarteng, Kwasi, 79, 107

Lawson, Nigel, 9, 95–97, 156n

Medium Term Financial Strategy
    (MTFS), 95, 106, 109
monetarism, 61, 67, 69–76, 151n,
    153n
    pragmatic monetarism,
        69–76

money supply growth, 7, 9, 11,
    52, 59–61, 63, 66–67,
    72–76, 81, 94, 96,
    119–121, 142
moral issues of inflation, xi, 31–34,
    36–37, 40, 47, 130–131,
    141, 150n
morality, 37, 47, 131–132
Moriarty, Clare (Dame), 148n
Morgan, Lord (Kenneth O.), 53,
    150n
multiculturalism, 133

Napoleonic Wars, 4, 5, 129, 147n
Nietzsche, Freidrich, 131, 138,
    156n, 157n
Nixon, Richard, 8, 12

Office for Budget Responsibility
    (OBR), 103–104, 106–109,
    113, 127–129, 143, 153n,
    154n, 156n
Office for National Statistics
    (ONS), 9, 24, 78, 148n,
    155n
O'Neill, Baroness (Onora), 47,
    150n

Phillips, A. W., 19, 60, 148n
    Phillips curve, 19, 20, 94
Pill, Huw, 82, 152n
pound sterling, 3, 7–8, 25,
    35–38, 46, 49, 97,
    106–107, 153n
price gouging and profiteering, 33,
    43, 88–89

public sector debt, 103, 108–109, 154n
Putin, Vladimir, 11, 43, 76

quantitative easing (QE), 11–12, 75, 78–79, 81–82, 142, 147n, 148n

radical uncertainty, x, 17, 82, 127–128, 142, 148n
Rajan, Raghuram, 121, 147, 152n, 156n
Reagan, Ronald, 46, 71, 73
regulation, 82, 110, 117, 118, 142
religion, 75, 130–131, 137–139, 143
Ricardo, David, 59, 61, 105, 119
risk, x, 17, 42, 74, 83, 103–104, 107, 115, 118, 120, 125, 127, 128, 134, 142–143, 153n, 156n
Robbins, Lord (Lionel), 31, 34, 141, 149n
Röpke, Wilhelm, 31, 33, 141, 149n
Russia, ix–x, 10–11, 17, 25, 46, 50, 62, 77, 83, 92

Sacred Canopy, 132, 137–139, 143, 157n
Sandbrook, Dominic, 51, 150n
Schwartz, Anna, 62, 63, 151n
Sentance, Andrew, 155n
Smith, Adam, 59, 61, 105, 119, 142, 154n
sociology, xiv, 51, 137

strikes, xi, 21, 43–44, 52, 54
Sunak, Rishi, 39, 88, 106, 135

tax, 5–7, 11, 15, 18, 20, 26, 29, 31, 33, 37–40, 46–47, 59, 60, 70, 89, 94–96
Thatcher, Margaret (Baroness), ix, 20, 71, 73, 97–98, 106, 145, 153n
Treasury Committee (Commons Select Committee), 87, 122, 135, 139, 155n
Trevelyan, G. H., 129–130, 156n
Truss, Liz, 79, 107, 109

Ukraine, ix, x, 3, 5, 9, 10–11, 17, 25, 31, 60, 72, 77, 82–83, 92, 112, 119
unemployment, ix, xi, 6, 19–21, 31, 51, 60, 62, 69, 71, 78, 91–95, 97, 98, 105, 112, 128, 141, 148n, 156n
United States, x, 3, 7–8, 12, 62–63, 76, 91–92, 111, 113, 118, 124, 130, 133, 135, 136, 151n
US Federal Reserve, x, 37, 44, 62–64, 73–74, 81, 89, 97, 119
  independence, 124
  Bank of Minneapolis, 64, 151n
  Bank of St. Louis, 148n

Vietnam War, 3, 7, 8, 17, 63
Volcker, Paul, 73–74, 97–98, 149n, 152n, 153n

Walters, Alan, 9, 64, 72, 95, 151n, 153n
Warburton, Peter, xiii, 62, 64, 65
Wilson, Harold, 8, 20, 53
Winter of Discontent, 54
Wolf, Martin, 136, 157n

Wood, Geoffrey, 7, 147n
World War I, 4–5, 7, 11, 17, 46, 96, 130
World War II, 3–4, 6–7, 9, 19, 36, 62, 91

Yeats, W. B., 49–50, 54–55

Complete list of CEME publications

Richard Turnbull, *Quaker Capitalism: Lessons for Today*, 2014.

Edward Carter, *God and Enterprise*, 2016.

Richard Turnbull (ed.), *The Challenge of Social Welfare: Seeking a New Consensus*, 2016.

Richard Turnbull, *The Moral Case for Asset Management*, 2016 (published jointly with New City Initiative).

Martin Schlag, *Business in Catholic Social Thought*, 2016.

Andrei Rogobete, *Ethics in Global Business*, 2016.

Ben Cooper, *The Economics of the Hebrew Scriptures*, 2017.

Lyndon Drake, *Capital Markets for the Good of Society*, 2017.

Richard Turnbull and Tim Weinhold (eds), *Making Capitalism Work for Everyone*, volume 1, 2017.

Richard Turnbull and Tim Weinhold (eds), *Making Capitalism Work for Everyone*, volume 2, 2017.

Richard Turnbull, *Understanding the Common Good*, 2017.

Andrei Rogobete, *The Challenges of Migration*, 2018.

Steven Morris, *Enterprise and Entrepreneurship: Doing Good Through the Local Church*, 2018.

Richard Turnbull, *Work as Enterprise: Recovering a Theology of Work*, 2019.

Edward Carter, *God and Competition: Towards a Positive Theology of Competitive Behaviour*, 2019.

Steven Morris, *The Business of God*, 2019.

Andrew Hartropp, *Corporate Executive Remuneration*, 2019.

Richard Turnbull (ed.), *The Economic and Social Teaching of the Hebrew Scriptures*, 2020.

Andrei Rogobete, *The UK Savings Crisis*, 2020.

Barbara Ridpath, *Ethics and Economics: Economics as Servant or Master?*, 2021.

Philip Booth, Kaetana Numa, Stephen Nakrosis and Richard Turnbull, *Government Debt: A Neglected Theme of Catholic Social Teaching*, 2021.

Richard Turnbull (ed.), *What Is the Value of Business? Results of Polling*, 2022.

John Kroencke, *Private Planning and the Great Estates: Lessons from London*, 2022.

Andrei Rogobete, *The Challenge of Artificial Intelligence: Responsibly Unlocking the Potential of AI*, 2023.

Richard Turnbull, *Is the Non-Executive Director Worth Saving?*, 2024

Brian Griffiths, *Inflation Is About More Than Money*, 2024.